W9-DDC-064

THE BOOK OF FUNNY SPORTS QUOTES

HUMOROUS SPORTS QUOTATIONS FOR SPORTS FANS EVERYWHERE

By M. Prefontaine

INTRODUCTION

As sports enthusiasts will know one of the most important part of sports is what the various participants say as much as what they actually do.

This can be the pre match mind games of adversaries, the insightful observations of commentators or the inane comment which reveals a profound stupidity which could only have been guessed at.

These quotes provide a wealth of humorous comments which embroider and enrich the playing and watching of sports bringing additional dimensions to the game.

This collection brings together the favorite quotes of the author from a range of sports. Some selections are current while many are from famous sportsmen and commentators of the past.

I hope that every sports fan, whatever their favorite sport, will enjoy this collection.

TABLE OF CONTENTS

CHAPTER 1: GENERAL

I hate all sports as rabidly as a person who likes sports hates common sense.
HL Mencken (1880 – 1956)

A sports journalist is someone who would if he could but he can't, so he tells who already know how they should.
Cliff Temple (1947 – 94)

The more violent the body contact of the sports you watch, the lower your class.
Paul Fussell (1924 – 2012)

Games are the last resort of those who do not know how to idle.
Robert Lynd (1879 – 1949)

If the bible has taught us nothing, and it hasn't, its that girls should stick to girls' sports, such as hot oil wrestling, foxy boxing and such and such.
Homer Simpson

Sports are the reason I am out of shape. I watch them all on TV.
Thomas Sowell (1930 -)

Sports are dangerous and tiring activities performed by people with whom I share nothing in common except to the right to trial by jury.
Fran Lebowitz (1950 -)

I always turn to the sports section first. The sport pages record people's accomplishments. The front page has nothing but people's failures.
Justice Earl Warren (1891 – 1974)

The difference between the old ballplayer and the new ballplayer is the jersey. The old ballplayer cared about the name on the front. The new ballplayer cares about the name on the back.
Steve Garvey (1948 -)

Being a professional is doing the things you love to do, on the days you don't feel like doing them.
Julius Erving (1950 -)

Men forget everything; women remember everything. That's why men need instant replays in sports. They've already forgotten what happened.
Rita Rudner

The trouble with referees is that they just don't care who wins.
Tom Canterbury

Jews aren't athletes. I love hockey but if you see a Jew on ice he is in the morgue.
Brad Garrett (1960 -)

Winning is a habit. Unfortunately, so is losing.
Vince Lombardi Jr. (1913 – 70)

If you make every game a life-and-death thing, you're going to have problems. You'll be dead a lot.
Dean Smith (1971 -)

Winning is overrated. The only time it is really important is in surgery and war.
Al McGuire (1928 – 2001)

If a tie is like kissing your sister, losing is like kissing your grandmother with her teeth out.
George Brett (1992 -)

Officials are the only guys who can rob you and then get a police escort out of the stadium.
Ron Bolton (1950 -)

All sports are games of inches.
Dick Ritger (1938 -)

My only feeling about superstition is that it's unlucky to be behind at the end of the game.
Duffy Daugherty (1915 – 87)

Serious sport has nothing to do with fair play. It is bound up with hatred, jealousy, boastfulness, disregard of all rules and sadistic pleasure in witnessing violence: in other words, it is war minus the shooting... there are quite enough real causes of trouble already, and we need not add to them by encouraging young men to kick each other on the shins amid the roars of infuriated spectators.
George Orwell (1903 – 50)

Of course I have played outdoor games. I once played dominoes in an open air café in Paris.
Oscar Wilde (1854 – 1900)

The Olympics. Not a sport but a several peculiar sports, each of which only commands your attention every four years, like a dental appointment.
Dan Jenkins (1929 -)

I was watching what I thought was sumo wrestling on the television for two hours before I realized it was darts.
Hattie Hayridge (1954 -)

Climb every mountain, ford every burn,
Suffer a thrombosis, end up in an urn.
Arthur Marshall (1910 – 89)

I am afraid I play no outdoor games except dominoes. I have sometimes played dominoes outside a French café.
Oscar Wilde (1854 – 1900)

Chapter 2: American Football

Being in politics is like being a football coach. You have to be smart enough to understand the game, and dumb enough to think it important.
Eugene McCarthy (1916 – 2005)

I may be dumb, but I'm not stupid
Terry Bradshaw (1948 -)

Losing the super bowl is worse than death. With death, you don't have to get up in the morning.
George Allen (1918 – 90)

Emotion is highly overrated in football. My wife Corky is emotional as hell but can't play football worth a damn.
John McKay (1965 -)

Sure, luck means a lot in football. Not having a good quarterback is bad luck.
Don Shula (1930 -)

If I drop dead tomorrow, at least I'll know I died in good health.
Bum Phillips (1923 – 2013)

I have two weapons; my arms, my legs and my brain.
Michael Vick (1980 -)

You guys line up alphabetically by height.
Bill Peterson (1920 -93)

He is the only man I ever saw who ran his own interference.
Steve Owen (1898 – 1964)

I'm a light eater. As soon as it's light, I start to eat
Art Donovan (1924 – 2013)

We're as clean as any team. We wash our hands before we hit anybody.
Nate Newton (1961 -)

Football is, after all, a wonderful way to get rid of your aggressions without going to jail for it.
Heywood Hale Broun (1918 – 2001)

Most football players are temperamental. That's 90 percent temper and 10 percent mental.
Doug Plank (1953 -)

Football combines the two worst things about America: it is violence punctuated by committee meetings.
George F. Will (1941 -)

Pro football is like nuclear warfare. There are no winners, only survivors.
Frank Gifford (1930 – 2015)

Football is not a contact sport; it's a collision sport. Dancing is a good example of a contact sport.
Duffy Daugherty (1915 – 87)

When I went to Catholic high school in Philadelphia, we just had one coach for football and basketball. He took all of us who turned out and had us run through a forest. The ones who ran into the trees were on the football team.
George Raveling (1937 -)

College football is a sport that bears the same relation to education that bullfighting does to agriculture.
Elbert Hubbard (1856 – 1915)

Football players, like prostitutes, are in the business of ruining their bodies for the pleasure of strangers.
Merle Kessler (1949 -)

I feel like I'm the best, but you're not going to get me to say that.
Jerry Rice (1962 -)

If you think about it, I've never held a job in my life. I went from being an NFL player to a coach to a broadcaster. I haven't worked a day in my life.
John Madden (1936 -)

Nobody in football should be called a genius. A genius is a guy like Norman Einstein.
Joe Theismann (1949 -)

I'm not allowed to comment on lousy officiating.
Jim Fink

Most of my clichés aren't original.
Chuck Knox (1932 -)

I wouldn't ever set out to hurt anyone deliberately unless it was important — like a league game.
Dick Butkus

If the Super Bowl is really the ultimate game, why do they play it again next year?
Duane Thomas (1947 -)

If I had gone into professional football the name Jerry Ford might have been a household word today.
President Gerald Ford (1913 – 2006)

Pressure is something you feel when you don't know what the hell you're doing.
Peyton Manning (1976 -)

In Montana, they renamed a town after an all-time great, Joe Montana. Well, a town in Massachusetts changed their name to honor my guy Terry Bradshaw — Marblehead.
Howie Long (1960 -)

If defensive linemen's IQs were 5 points lower, they'd be geraniums.
Russ Francis (1953 -)

My knees look like they lost a knife fight with a midget.
E.J. Holub (1938 -)

I don't know what he has. A pulled groin. A hip flexor. I don't know. A pulled something. I never pulled anything. You can't pull fat.
Bruce Coslet (1946 -)

I like to believe that my best hits border on felonious assault.
Jack Tatum (1948 – 2010)

If you're a pro coach, NFL stands for Not For Long.
Jerry Glanville (1941 -)

He can be a great player in this league if he learns how to say two words: I'm full.
Jerry Glanville (1941 -)

What's the difference between a 3-week-old puppy and a sportswriter? In six weeks, the puppy stops whining.
Mike Ditka (1939 -)

It's almost exciting to think about all the room for improvement that we have.
Geno Smith (1990 -)

Well, we've determined that we can't win at home and we can't win on the road. What we need is a neutral site.
John Mc Kay (1923 – 2001)

The NFL is, like life, full of idiots.
Randy Cross (1954 -)

CHAPTER 3: ARCHERY

Time flies like an arrow - but fruit flies like a banana.
Groucho Marx (1890 – 1977)

I love archery because it prepares me for the zombie apocalypse.
Anon

The only way I can get my arrows to group is to keep them in my quiver.
Anon

The archer that shoots badly has a lie ready.
Spanish Proverb

You are the bows from which your children as living arrows are sent forth.
Kahlil Gibran (1883 – 1931)

I think therefore I miss.
Anon

Thought is the arrow of time; memory never fades.
Robert Jordan (1948 – 2007)

No shot is hard to make, it's just easier to miss
Anon

To be sure of hitting the target, shoot first and, whatever you hit, call it the target.
Ashleigh Brilliant (1933 -)

Death is like an arrow that is already in flight, and your life lasts only until it reaches you.
Georg Hermes (1775 – 1831)

Just as an arrow once released from the bow cannot return, in the same manner painful and harsh words cannot be taken back.
Samaveda

Archery does not get difficult or hard to understand until the arrow misses.
Milan E. Elott (1913 – 81)

I shoot an arrow into the air, where it lands I do not care: I get my arrows wholesale!
Curly Howard (1903 – 51)

Draw not your bow till your arrow is fixed.
English Proverb

The more expensive gadgets you put on your bow, the more possibilities you have for excuses.
Anon

An archer's creativeness for excuses is only limited by the number of arrows in their quiver.
Anon

Paid for a whole target, I use the whole target
Anon

CHAPTER 4: ATHLETICS

Behind every good decathlete, there's a good doctor.
Bill Toomey (1939 -)

If God invented marathons to keep people from doing anything more stupid, the triathlon must have taken Him completely by surprise.
P.Z. Pearce

I believe that every human being has a finite number of heartbeats, and I don't intend to waste any of mine running around doing exercises.
Neil Armstrong (1930 – 2012)

Seb Coe is a Yorkshireman. So he's a complete bastard and will do well in politics.
Daley Thompson (1958 -)

You have to be suspicious when you line up against girls with moustaches.
Maree Holland (1963 -)

And the hush of anticipation is rising to a crescendo.
Ron Pickering (1930 – 91)

Ben Johnson must still be the fastest human in the world. He served a lifetime sentence in just two years.
Mike Littwin

I don't think the discus will ever attract any interest until they let us start throwing them at one another.
Al Carter (1952 -)

If you want to know what you'll look like in ten years, look in the mirror after you've run a marathon.
Jeff Scaff

Italian men and Russian women don't shave before a race.
Eddie Ottoz (1944 -)

A cross-country runner is a landscape panter.
Anon

I was not talented enough to run and smile at the same time.
Emil Zatopek (1922 – 2000)

I became a great runner because if you're a kid in Leeds and your name is Sebastian you've got to become a great runner.
Sebastian Coe (1956 -)

The only reason I would take up jogging is so that I could hear heavy breathing again.
Erma Bombeck (1927 – 96)

The trouble with jogging is that by the time you realize you're not in shape for it, it's too far to walk back.
Franklin Jones

Most people never run far enough on their first wind to find out they've got a second.
William James (1842 – 1910)

Pain is inevitable. Suffering is optional.
Haruki Murakami (1949 -)

Life is short, running makes it seem longer.
Baron Hansen (1922 – 2004)

The great thing about athletics is that it's like poker sometimes: you know what's in your hand, and it may be a load of rubbish, but you've got to keep up the front.
Sebastian Coe (1956 -)

Run when you can, walk if you have to, crawl if you must; just never give up.
Dean Karnazes (1962 -)

A very powerful set of lungs, very much hidden by that chest of his.
Alan Pascoe (1947 -)

Being a decathlete is like having ten girlfriends. You have to love them all, and you can't afford losing one.
Daley Thompson (1958 -)

I spent 12 years training for a career that was over in one week. Joe Namath [New York Jets] spent one week training for a career that lasted 12 years.
Bruce Jenner (1949 -)

When I lost my decathlon world record I took it like a man. I only cried for ten hours.
Daley Thompson (1958 -)

I always wanted to be a minor poet. I remember when I did my record long jump saying to myself, when I was in the air half-way, 'This may be pretty good jumping. It's dashed poor minor poetry!'
C. B. Fry (1872 – 1956)

I know I'm no Kim Basinger, but she can't throw a javelin.
Fatima Whitbread (1961 -)

In a moment, we hope to see the pole vault over the satellite.
David Coleman (1926 – 2013)

Mention that you are a hammer thrower to someone who is not an athletics enthusiast and you will be met with any reaction from a puzzled frown to raucous laughter. If you have the misfortune to say it to a groundsman, you may face physical violence.
Howard Payne

They may have helped Linford Christie shave a millisecond or-two off his personal best but not everyone is Linford Christie. And contour-hugging cycle shorts can cruelly expose anyone whose performance falls an inch or two short of an all-comers' record. You need a full kitbag to get away with this particular garb. That might explain why so many men wear their cycle shorts under their regular strip.
Richard Littlejohn (1954 -)

To be number one, you have to train like your number two.
Maurice Greene (1974 -)

I don't think jogging is healthy, especially morning jogging. If morning joggers knew how tempting they looked to morning motorists, they would stay home and do sit-ups.
Rita Rudner (1953 -)

I used to jog but the ice cubes kept falling out of my glass.
David Lee Roth (1954 -)

If you think running a marathon is hard, try giving birth.
Anon

Why am I returning to Brooklyn? Because I love to wake up to garbage trucks and gunshots.
Diane Dixon (1964 -)

It's obvious these Russian swimmers are determined to do well on American soil
Anita Lonsborough (1941 -)

Jogging is for people who aren't intelligent enough to watch breakfast TV.
Victoria Wood (1953 -)

I go running when I have to. When the ice cream truck is doing sixty.
Wendy Liebman (1961 -)

CHAPTER 5: BASEBALL

You can sum up the game of baseball in one word: 'You never know'.
Joaquin Andujar (1952 – 2015)

You know what I love best about baseball? The pine tar, the resin, the grass, the dirt – and that's just I the hot dogs.
David Letterman (1947 -)

A friend got me seats for the World Series. From where I sat the game was just a rumor.
Henry Youngman (1906 – 98)

I like my players to be married and in debt. That's the way you motivate them.
Ernie Banks (1931 – 2015)

More than any other American sport, baseball creates the magnetic, addictive illusion that it can almost be understood.
Thomas Boswell (1947 -)

Any pitcher who deliberately throws at a batter's head is a Communist.
Alvin Dark (1922-2014)

He's got power enough to hit home-runs in any park, including Yellowstone.
Sparky Anderson (1934 – 2010)

When we (England) have a World Series we ask other countries to participate.
John Cleese (1939 -)

The doctors x-rayed my head and found nothing.
Dizzy Dean (1910 – 74)

If it is true you learn by your mistakes Jim Frey will be the best manager ever.
Ron Luciano (1937 – 95)

Pudge (Fisk) is so old they didn't have history class when he went to school.
Steve Lyons (1960 -)

Could be Bill Terry's a nice guy when you get to know him, but why bother?
Dizzy Dean (1910 – 74)

Winning is the most important thing in my life, after breathing. Breathing first, winning next.
George Steinbrenner (1930 – 2010)

Ryan Roberts has so many tattoos he looks like he got drunk and passed out in a comic book factory.
Greg Tamblyn

Good pitching will beat good hitting any time, and vice versa.
Bob Veale (1935 -)

People ask me what I do in winter when there's no baseball. I'll tell you what I do. I stare out the window and wait for spring.
Rogers Hornsby (1896 – 1963)

Baseball is the only field of endeavor where a man can succeed three times out of ten and be considered a good performer.
Ted Williams (1918 – 2002)

I never questioned the integrity of an umpire. Their eyesight, yes.
Leo Durocher (1905 – 91)

I was thinking of making a comeback till I pulled a muscle vacuuming.
Johnny Bench (1947 -)

I occasionally get birthday cards from fans. But often it's the same message. They hope it's my last.
Al Forman, former umpire (1928- 2013)

The only thing my father and I have in common is that our similarities are different.
Dale Berra (1956 -)

Garry Maddox has turned his life around. He used to be depressed and miserable. Now he is miserable and depressed.
Harry Kalas (1936 – 09)

A critic once characterized baseball as six minutes of action crammed into two-and-one-half hours.
Ray Fitzgerald (1904 – 77)

Things could be worse. Suppose your errors were counted and published every day, like those of a baseball player.
Anon

We've made too many wrong mistakes.
Yogi Berra (1925 – 15)

There has never been a question over his courage. He has proved it by getting married four times.
Jack Brickhouse (1916 – 98)

Baseball is an island of activity amidst a sea of statistics.
Anon

Baseball is like church. Many attend, few understand.
Leo Durocher (1905 – 91)

I can remember a sports writer asking me for a quote and I didn't know what a quote was. I thought it was some kind of soft drink.
Joe DiMaggio (1914 – 99)

Ninety percent of this game is half mental.
Yogi Berra (1925 – 15)

The average age of our bench is deceased.
Tommy Lasorda (1927 -)

I have discovered in 20 years of moving around a ballpark, that the knowledge of the game is usually in inverse proportion to the price of the seats.
Bill Veeck (1914 -86)

If it turns out that Barry Bonds used steroids to bulk up and add muscle mass, he could get 4 to 8 years as governor of California.
Argus Hamilton (1951 -)

Baseball hasn't forgotten me. I go to a lot of old-timers games and I haven't lost a thing. I sit in the bullpen and let people throw things at me. Just like old times.
Bob Uecker (1934 -)

Baseball is almost the only orderly thing in a very unorderly world. If you get three strikes, even the best lawyer in the world can't get you off.
Bill Veeck (1914 -86)

I hated to bat against Drysdale. After he hit you he'd come around, look at the bruise on your arm and say, 'Do you want me to sign it?'
Mickey Mantle (1931 – 95)

I walk into the clubhouse today and it's like walking into the Mayo Clinic. We have four doctors, three therapists and five trainers. Back when I broke in, we had one trainer who carried a bottle of rubbing alcohol, and by the 7th inning he'd already drunk it.
Tommy Lasorda (1927 -)

I hit a grand slam off Ron Herbel. And when his manager, Herman Franks, came out to get him, he brought Herbel's suitcase.
Bob Uecker (1934 -)

The coach put me in right field only because it was against the rules to put me in Sweden, where I would have done less damage to the team.
Dave Barry (1947 -)

The Angels could take batting practice in a hotel lobby and not break the chandelier.
Bill Lee (1946 -)

For the parents of a Little Leaguer, a baseball game is simply a nervous breakdown divided into innings.
Earl Wilson (1907 – 87)

There are only two seasons—winter and baseball.
Bill Veeck (1914 – 86)

If a woman has to choose between catching a fly ball and saving an infant's life, she will choose to save the infant's life without even considering if there are men on base.
Dave Barry (1947 -)

During my 18 years I came to bat almost 10,000 times. I struck out about 1,700 times and walked maybe 1,800 times. You figure a ballplayer will average about 500 at bats a season. That means I played seven years without ever hitting the ball.
Mickey Mantle (1931 – 95)

Hitting is timing. Pitching is upsetting timing.
Warren Spahn (1921 – 2003)

Hating the New York Yankees is as American as apple pie, unwed mothers and cheating on your income tax.
Mike Royko (1932 – 97)

Playing baseball for a living is like having a license to steal.
Pete Rose (1941 -)

If people don't want to come out to the ball park no one is going to stop them.
Yogi Berra (1925 – 15)

Baseball is very big with my people. It figures. It's the only way we can get to shake a bat at a white man without starting a riot.
Dick Gregory (1932 -)

All you have to do is to keep the five players who hate your guts away from the five who are undecided.
Casey Stengel (1890 – 75)

Baseball, it is said, is only a game. True. And the Grand Canyon is only a hole in Arizona. Not all holes, or games, are created equal.
George F Will (1941 -)

CHAPTER 6: BASKETBALL

I'm in favour of drug tests, just so long as they are multiple choice.
Kurt Rambis (1958 -)

Manute Bol is so skinny, they save money on road trips – they just fax him from city to city.
Woody Allen (1935 -)

If you can walk with your head in the clouds and keep your feet on the ground, you can make a million dollars in the NBA.
Gary Dornhoefer (1943 -)

If cocaine were helium, the NBA would float away.
Art Rust (1927 – 2010)

We don't need referees in basketball, but it gives the white guys something to do.
Charles Barkley (1963 -)

We can't win at home. We can't win on the road. As general manager, I just can't figure out where else to play.
Pat Williams (1940 -)

I never thought I'd lead the NBA in rebounding, but I got a lot of help from my team-mates - they did a lot of missing.
Moses Malone (1955 – 2015)

I told him, 'Son, what is it with you? Is it ignorance or apathy?' He said, 'Coach, I don't know and I don't care.'
Frank Layden (1932 -)

What is so fascinating about sitting around watching a bunch of pituitary cases stuff a ball through a hoop?
Woody Allen (1935 -)

A team should be an extension of a coach's personality. My teams are arrogant and obnoxious.
Al McGuire (1928 – 2001)

Finish last in your league and they call you "idiot." Finish last in medical school and they call you "doctor."
Abe Lemons (1922 – 2002)

The NBA is like a small sorority. We're like brothers.
Rashad Lewis (1979 -)

We're going to turn this team around 360 degrees.
Jason Kidd (1973 -)

They say that nobody is perfect. Then they tell you practice makes perfect. I wish they'd make up their minds.
Wilt Chamberlain (1936 – 99)

If I weren't earning $3 million a year to dunk a basketball, most people on the street would run in the other direction if they saw me coming.
Charles Barkley (1963 -)

Any American boy can be a basketball star if he grows up, up, up.
Bill Vaughn (1915 – 77)

If you make every game a life and death proposition, you're going to have problems. For one thing, you'll be dead a lot.
Dean Smith (1931 – 2015)

Good, better, best. Never let it rest. Until your good is better and your better is best.
Tim Duncan (1976 -)

I only know how to play two ways: reckless and abandon.
Earvin 'Magic' Johnson (1959 -)

In my prime I could have handled Michael Jordan. Of course, he would be only 12 years old.
Jerry Sloan (1942 -)

Basketball is like photography, if you don't focus, all you have is the negative.
Dan Frisby

Basketball has so much showboating you'd think it was invented by Jerome Kern.
Art Spander (1940 -)

Left hand, right hand, it doesn't matter. I'm amphibious.
Charles Shackleford (1966 -)

There are some remarkable parallels between basketball and politics. Michael Jordan has already mastered the skill most needed for political success: how to stay aloft without visible means of support.
Margaret Thatcher (1925 – 2013)

I'm tired of hearing about money, money, money, money, money. I just want to play the game, drink Pepsi, wear Reebok.
Shaquille O'Neal (1972 -)

This [basketball] is the second most exciting indoor sport, and the other one shouldn't have spectators.
Dick Vertlieb (1930 – 2008)

The trouble with officials is they just don't care who wins.
Tommy Canterbury (1957 -)

Mick Jagger is in better shape than far too many NBA players. It's up in the air whether the same can be said of Keith Richards.
Bill Walton (1952 -)

The secret is to have eight great players and four others who will cheer like crazy.
Jerry Tarkanian (1930 – 2015)

I haven't been able to slam-dunk the basketball for the past five years. Or, for the thirty-eight years before that, either.
Dave Barry (1947 -)

I've never had major knee surgery on any other part of my body.
Winston Bennett (1965 -)

Nobody roots for Goliath.
Wilt Chamberlain (1936 – 99)

I'm a coach who believes in execution. Whenever I see [that player] shoot free throws, I want to execute him.
Rick Pitino (1952 -)

I wouldn't bank on it. I would still say, right now, he's probably doubtful, but that could become questionable. But I don't think it's probable.
Bill Self (1962 -)

Jeremy Lin may be the first person with an economics degree from Harvard who is doing something positive with his life.
Andy Borowitz (1958 -)

I always mean what I say, but I don't always say what I'm thinking.
Dean Smith (1931 – 2015)

It is foolish to expect a young man to follow your advice and to ignore your example.
Don Meyer (1944 – 2014)

When opportunity comes, it's too late to prepare.
John Wooden (1920 – 2010)

I can be bought. If they paid me enough, I'd work for the Klan.
Charles Barkley (1963 -)

All I know is, as long as I led the Southeastern Conference in scoring, my grades would be fine.
Charles Barkley (1963 -)

Sometimes you're the pigeon, and sometimes you're the statue.
Bernie Bickerstaff (1944 -)

I hate it. It looks like a stickup at 7-Eleven. Five guys standing there with their hands in the air.
Norm Sloan (1926 – 2003)

The first time I saw Dick Vitale, his hair was blowing in the breeze. And he was too proud to chase it.
Cliff Ellis (1945 -)

They had so many injuries they had to park their bu in the handicapped zone.
George Raveling (1937 -)

I've got to stop this. My entourage is getting entourages.
Jalen Rose (1973 -)

I asked a referee if he would give me a technical foul for thinking bad things about him. He said 'Of course not'. I said, 'Well I think you stink'. And he gave me a technical. You can't trust 'em.
Jim Valvano (1946 – 93)

We were so bad last year the cheerleaders stayed at home and phoned in their cheers.
Pat Williams (1940 -)

Manute Bol is so thin his pajamas have only one pinstripe.
Pat Williams (1940 -)

When the list of great coaches is finally read out, I believe Frank Layden will be there...listening.
Pat Williams (1940 -)

CHAPTER 7: BOWLING

I could be a trophy hubby. I have the body of an elite athlete...that of a pro bowler.
Jarod Kintz (1982 -)

I can't believe I've missed this sport. It's all about fingering holes and caressing balls.
K.A. Mitchell

One of the advantages bowling has over golf is that you seldom lose a bowling ball.
Don Carter (1926 - 2012)

I am not an athlete, more a gymnast and a golfer soldered together.
David Bryant (1931 -)

Having children is like having a bowling alley installed in your brain.
Martin Mull (1943 -)

Oh, come on, I love bowling! It's the perfect workout. Six seconds of exercise, drink beer half an hour.
Roseanne Connor

Listen Jerry, bowling is a man's sport. If God had wanted women to bowl, he would have put their breasts on their backs so we would have something to watch while waiting our turn.
Al Bundy

Ah, the alleys . . . It's really a sensory experience, you know. The scent of Aqua Net on a beehive hairdo. The roar of polyester rubbing against old Naugahyde. The site of a cigarette stubbed out on a patty melt. All this plus the anticipation of placing your feet in shoes only seven thousand others have worn before you.
Diane Chambers

Amateurs move it right to left, and pros move it front to back.
Del Ballard (1963 -)

The bowling alley is the poor man's country club.
Sanford Hansell

If only Hitler and Mussolini could have a good game of bowls once a week at Geneva, I feel that Europe would not be as troubled as it is.
R.G. Briscow

CHAPTER 8: BOXING

The same hand that can write a beautiful poem, can knock you out with one punch—that's Poetic Justice.
Wayne Kelly (1948 - 2012)

I quit school in the sixth grade because of pneumonia. Not because I had it but because I couldn't spell it.
Rocky Graziano (1919 – 90)

I've often wondered why boxing gloves are bright red. If I were a boxer, I'd wear camouflage colored boxing gloves so my opponent would never see my punches coming.
Jarod Kintz (1982 -)

I was in a no-win situation, so I'm glad that I won rather than lost.
Frank Bruno (1961 -)

To me, boxing is like a ballet - except there's no music, no choreography, and the dancers hit each other.
Jack Handey (1949 -)

A computer once beat me at chess, but it was no match for me at kick boxing.
Emo Philips (1956 -)

I've seen George Foreman shadow boxing, and the shadow won.
Muhammad Ali (1942 -)

The dumbest question I was ever asked by a sportswriter was whether I hit harder with red or white gloves. As a matter of fact, I hit harder with red.
Frank Crawford (1870 - 1963)

Lie down so I can recognise you.
Willie Pep (1922 - 2006)

The right cross-counter is distinctly one of those things which is more blessed to give than to receive.
P. G. Wodehouse (1881 - 1975)

Journalist Howard Cosell was going to be a boxer when he was a kid, only they couldn't find a mouthpiece big enough.
Muhammad Ali (1942 -)

The noise that comes from the wretched throats of a boxing crowd indicates that brain damage is also in the head of the beholder.
Julie Burchill (1959 -)

You know why Mike Tyson's eyes water when he's having sex? Mace.
John Caponera (195 9-)

Chris Eubank lost his recent comeback fight on points ... the main one being that he's a total git.
Nick Hancock (1962 -)

Before Don King started insulting me I was a complete unknown in this country. Now people stop me and ask for my autograph.
Frank Maloney (1953 -)

They told me Jack Bodell was awkward and he was ... he fell awkwardly.
Jerry Quarry (1945 - 1999)

I got into the ring with Muhammad Ali once and I had him worried for a while. He thought he'd killed me!
Tommy Cooper (1921 – 84)

If the Bible has taught us nothing else, and it hasn't, it's that girls should stick to girls' sports, such as hot oil wrestling, foxy boxing, and such and such.
Homer Simpson

Boxing is just show business with blood.
Frank Bruno (1961 -)

This is America. It's different. It is not like England, where you can fight a tuna fish and get $3m.
Kevin Kelley (1968 -)

When you can count your money you ain't got none.
Don King (1931 -)

They say money talks but the only thing it ever said to me was goodbye.
Joe Louis (1914 - 1981)

I have got it made. I have got a wife and a TV set – and they are both working.
Willie Pep (1922 - 2006)

Prize fighters can sometimes read and write when they start — but they can't when they finish.
Martin H. Fischer (1879 - 1962)

He called me a rapist and a recluse. I'm not a recluse.
Mike Tyson (1966 -)

If they can make penicillin out of mouldy bread, then they can sure make something out of you.
Muhammad Ali (1942 -)

Never Fight ugly people—they have nothing to Lose.
Wayne Kelly

Why would anyone expect him to come out smarter? He went to prison for three years, not Princeton.
Dan Duva (1951 - 1996)

All the time he's boxing, he's thinking. All the time he was thinking, I was hitting him.
Jack Dempsey (1895 - 1983)

If you even dream of beating me you'd better wake up and apologize.
Muhammad Ali (1942 -)

It's just a job. Grass grows, birds fly, waves pound the sand. I beat people up.
Muhammad Ali (1942 -)

Years ago we had the Raging Bull, Jake LaMotta. Today, we've got the Raging Bullshit, Bruce Strauss.
Teddy Brenner (1918 – 2000)

After Lennox Lewis lost his world title to Oliver McCall- Lennox Lewis has two chances of getting a rematch with McCall - no chance and slim. And slim has just left town.
Don King (1931 -)

Las Vegas is the oasis of outstretched palms.
Reg Gutteridge (1924 - 2009)

He's not only a lousy fighter, he's a bad actor. Louis or Marciano could have whipped him by telephone.
Dan Digilio

Never in the ring of human conflict have so few taken so much from so many.
Saoul Mamby (1947 -)

The question isn't at what age I want to retire, it's at what income.
George Foreman (1949 -)

I'll beat him so bad he'll need a shoehorn to put his hat on.
Muhammad Ali (1942 -)

My day starts like a regular guy's. I wake up, drink raw eggs, run around Philadelphia, and punch raw slabs of meat. Wait, that's not my story—that's Rocky's. I get us confused all the time.
Jarod Kintz (1982 -)

Boxing is the only sport you can get your brain shook, your money took and your name in the undertaker book.
Joe Frazier (1944 - 2011)

The bum was up and down so many times I thought he was an Otis elevator.
Harry Kabakoff (1927 – 2009)

Boxers, like prostitutes, are in the business of ruining their bodies for the pleasure of strangers.
Wayne Kelly (1948 – 2012)

Boxing is a lot of white men watching two black men beat each other up.
Muhammad Ali (1942 -)

We are all endowed with God given talents. Mine happens to be hitting people in the head.
Sugar Ray Leonard (1956 -)

I miss things like the camaraderie in the gym. I don't miss being smacked in the mouth every day.
Barry McGuigan (1961 -)

CHAPTER 9: CHESS

The good thing in chess is that very often the best moves are the most beautiful ones. The beauty of logic.
Boris Gelfand (1968 -)

Chess is the most elaborate waste of human intelligence that you can find outside of an advertising agency.
Raymond Chandler (1888 – 1958)

I had lunch with a chess champion the other day. I knew he was a chess champion because he took twenty minutes to pass the salt.
Eric Sykes (1923 – 2012)

A Chess game is divided into three stages: the first, when you hope you have the advantage, the second when you believe you have an advantage, and the third... when you know you're going to lose!
Savielly Tartakower (1887 – 1956)

No Chess Grandmaster is normal; they only differ in the extent of their madness.
Viktor Korchnoi (1931 -)

Marriage is like a game of chess except the board is flowing water, the pieces are made of smoke and no move you make will have any effect on the outcome.
Jerry Seinfeld (1954 -)

Most gods throw dice, but Fate plays chess, and you don't find out till too late that he's been playing with two queens all along.
Terry Pratchett (1948 – 2015)

Chess is ruthless: you've got to be prepared to kill people.
Nigel Short (1965 -)

I'm like Bush, I see the world more like checkers than chess.
Dennis Miller (1953 -)

Chess is a sea in which a gnat may drink and an elephant may bathe.
Indian proverb

The tactician knows what to do when there is something to do; whereas the strategian knows what to do when there is nothing to do.
Gerald Abrahams (1907 – 80)

The chessboard is the world, the pieces are the phenomena of the Universe, the rules of the game are what we call the laws of Nature and the player on the other side is hidden from us.
Thomas Huxley (1825 – 95)

Strategy requires thought, tactics require observation.
Max Euwe (1901 – 81)

If cunning alone were needed to excel, women would be the best Chess players.
Adolf Albin (1848 – 1920)

If your opponent offers you a draw, try to work out why he thinks he's worse off.
Nigel Short (1965 -)

You must take your opponent into a deep dark forest where 2+2=5, and the path leading out is only wide enough for one.
Mikhail Tal (1936 – 92)

What is the object of playing a gambit opening?... To acquire a reputation of being a dashing player at the cost of losing a game.
Siegbert Tarrasch (1862 – 1934)

There are two classes of men; those who are content to yield to circumstances and who play whist; those who aim to control circumstances, and who play chess.
Mortimer Collins (1827 – 96)

A man that will take back a move at Chess will pick a pocket.
Richard Fenton (1837 – 1916)

Those who say they understand Chess, understand nothing.
Robert Hubner (1948 -)

In life, unlike chess, the game continues after checkmate.
Isaac Asimov (1992 -)

A computer once beat me at chess, but it was no match for me at kick boxing.
Emo Philips (1956 -)

I failed to make the chess team because of my height.
Woody Allen (1935 -)

There is nothing that disgusts a man like getting beaten at chess by a woman.
Charles Dudley Warner (1829 – 1900)

Life's too short for chess.
Henry James Byron (1835 – 1884)

[Chess] is a foolish expedient for making idle people believe they are doing something very clever, when they are only wasting their time.
George Bernard Shaw (1856 – 1950)

In chess, as a purely intellectual game, where randomness is excluded, - for someone to play against himself is absurd ... It is as paradoxical, as attempting to jump over his own shadow.
Stefan Zweig (1881 – 1942)

My favorite victory is when it is not even clear where my opponent made a mistake.
Peter Leko (1979 -)

Chess is not like life... it has rules!
Mark Pasternak

Chess is in its essence a game, in its form an art, and in its execution a science.
Baron Tassilo (1818 – 99)

Every Pawn is a potential Queen.
James Mason (1849 – 1905)

Chess is mental torture.
Gary Kasparov (1963 -)

When your house is on fire, you can't be bothered with the neighbors. Or, as we say in Chess, if your King is under attack you don't worry about losing a Pawn on the Queen's side.
Gary Kasparov (1963 -)

Man is a frivolous, a specious creature, and like a Chess player, cares more for the process of attaining his goal than for the goal itself.
Fyodor Dostoyevsky (1821 – 81)

All Chess players should have a hobby.
Savielly Tartakower (1887 – 1956)

If Chess is a science, it's a most inexact one. If Chess is an art, it is too exacting to be seen as one. If Chess is a sport, it's too esoteric. If Chess is a game, it's too demanding to be just a game. If Chess is a mistress, she's a demanding one. If Chess is a passion, it's a rewarding
one. If Chess is life, it's a sad one
Anon

CHAPTER 10: CRICKET

A cricket tour in Australia would be a most delightful period in one's life if one was deaf.
Harold Larwood (1904 - 1995)

I watched a cricket match for three hours waiting for it to start.
Groucho Marx (1890 – 1977)

Before the IPL, the girls who I used to message didn't care to reply. After the IPL, the same girls started messaging me every day. After that I stopped talking to them.
Shreyas Iyer (1994 -)

He played a cut so late as to be positively posthumous.
John Arlott (1914 - 1991)

Tufnell! Can I borrow your brain? I'm building an idiot.
Australian fan

England trained and grass grew at the MCG yesterday, two activities virtually indistinguishable from each other in tempo.
Greg Baum (1959 -)

The other advantage England have got when Phil Tufnell is bowling is that he isn't fielding.
Ian Chappell (1943 -)

Ian Botham is in no way inhibited by a capacity to over-intellectualise.
Frances Edmonds

Boycott and controversy have shared the longest opening partnership in the game.
Terry Brindle (1946 -)

Bill [Frindall] needs a small ruler. How about the Sultan of Brunei? I hear he is only four foot ten.
Brian Johnston (191 2- 1994)

This bowler's like my dog: three short legs and balls which swing each way.
Brian Johnston (1912 - 1994)

An oyster bar - apparently it puts lead in your pencil. I don't know about that. I think it only matters if you have got someone to write to.
David Lloyd (1947 -)

Andre Nel is big and raw-boned and I suspect he has the IQ of an empty swimming pool.
Adam Parore (1971 -)

Bill Lawry is a corpse with pads on.
Anon

It is rather suitable that umpires dress like dentists, since one of their tasks is to draw stumps.
John Arlott (1914 - 1991)

Cricket is a game played by 11 fools and watched by 11,000 fools.
George Bernard Shaw (1856 - 1950)

If you make a team with all the No.11s of all the teams, Hirwani would still come at No.11 in the lineup.
Harsha Bhogle (1961 -)

The only time an Australian ever walks is when his car runs out of petrol.
Barry Richards (1945 -)

How anyone can spin a ball the width of Gatting boggles the mind.
Martin Johnson

Neil Harvey's at slip, with his legs wide apart, waiting for a tickle.
Brian Johnston (1912 - 1994)

The hallmark of a great captain is the ability to win the toss at the right time.
Richie Benaud (1930 - 2015)

It kind of felt like I was the library in a theme park.
Kane Williamson (1990 -)

Gym. Like dancing, holding hands, queueing. Overrated.
Shane Warne (1969 -)

Getting a hundred in 31 balls was unheard of. I took 31 balls to get off the mark.
Sunil Gavaskar (1949 -)

Strangely, in slow motion, the ball seemed to hang in the air for even longer.
David Acfield (1947 -)

I once delivered a simple ball, which I was told, had it gone far enough, would have been considered a wide.
Lewis Carroll (1832 - 1898)

I can't really say I'm batting badly. I'm not batting long enough to be batting badly.
Greg Chappell (1948 -)

This is Cunis at the Vauxhall End. Cunis—a funny sort of name. Neither one thing nor the other.
Alan Gibson (1923 - 1997)

Being the manager of a touring team is rather like being in charge of a cemetery - lots of people underneath you, but no one listening.
Wes Hall (1937 -)

What do I think of the reverse sweep? It's like Manchester United getting a penalty and Bryan Robson taking it with his head.
David Lloyd (1947 -)

The third umpires should be changed as often as nappies... and for the same reason.
Navjot Sidhu (1963 -)

For those of you who are wondering what that round of applause (by Edgbaston crowd) was, it was to mark the resignation of Ted Dexter.
Johnathan Agnew (1960 -)

England have only three major problems. They can't bat, they can't bowl and they can't field.
Martin Johnson

Welcome to Leicester where the captain Ray Illingworth has just relieved himself at the Pavilion End.
Brian Johnston (1912 - 1994)

As he comes into bowl, Freddie Titmus has got two short legs, one of them square.
Brian Johnston (1912 - 1994)

It couldn't have been Gatt. Anything he takes up to his room after nine o'clock, he eats.
Ian Botham (1955 -)

Merv Hughes always appeared to be wearing a tumble-dried ferret on his top lip.
Rick Broadbent

Gatting at fine leg - that's a contradiction in terms.
Richie Benaud (1930 - 2015)

It's a funny kind of month, October. For the really keen cricket fan it's when you discover that your wife left you in May.
Denis Norden (1922-)

I need nine wickets from this game, and you buggers better start drawing straws to see who I don't get.
Fred Trueman (1931 - 2006)

I cannot for the life of me see why the umpires, the only two people on a cricket field who are not going to get grass stains on their knees, are the only two people allowed to wear dark trousers.
Katharine Whitehorn (1928 -)

Life is simply a cricket match, with temptation as the bowler.
Anon

Henry Horton has a funny stance. It looks as though he is shitting on a sooting stick.
Brian Johnston (1912 - 1994)

I'm confident they play the game in heaven. Wouldn't be heaven otherwise would it?
Patrick Moore (1923 - 2012)

Chapter 11: Cycling

Wind is just a hill in gaseous form.
Barry McCarty (1953 -)

And he's out there in front breaking wind for the rest of the peloton.
Phil Liggett (1943 -)

When I was a kid I used to pray every night for a new bicycle. Then I realised that the Lord doesn't work that way so I stole one and asked Him to forgive me.
Emo Philips (1956 -)

Give a man a fish and feed him for a day. Teach a man to fish and feed him for a lifetime. Teach a man to cycle and he will realize fishing is stupid and boring.
Desmond Tutu (1931 -)

I would rather weep in a Rolls-Royce than be happy on a bicycle.
Patrizia Reggiani (1948 -)

What do you call a cyclist who doesn't wear a helmet? An organ donor.
David Perry (1967 -)

No wonder we keep testing positive in their bicycle races. Everyone looks like they're full of testosterone when they're surrounded by Frenchmen.
Argus Hamilton (1951 -)

Marriage, Weekend Riding, Happiness - Choose Two
Anon

There's something wrong with a society that drives a car to go workout at the gym.
Bill Nye (1955 -)

The bicycle is just as good company as most husbands and, when it gets old and shabby, a woman can dispose of it and get a new one without shocking the entire community.
Ann Strong

Never use your face as a brake pad.
Jake Watson (1973 -99)

Get a bicycle. You will certainly not regret it, if you live.
Mark Twain (1835 – 1910)

There may be a better land where bicycle saddles are made of rainbow, stuffed with cloud; in this world the simplest thing is to get used to something hard.
Jerome K. Jerome (1859 – 1927)

A woman needs a man like a fish needs a bicycle.
Irina Dunn (1948 -)

I'm the paté on the Universal cracker. I'm the grout holding your shower tiles on. I'm out of the saddle, sprinting up that hill and eating glazed donut bracelets off the right arm of Jesus.
Charles Manson (1934 -)

What I'm sayin is, it's obvious, if ya don't push on the pedals the wheels won't turn.
George W Bush (1946 -)

The world is my church, the wind in my ears is the choir and my handlebars are the altar I pray at.
Anon

It's depressing when a butterfly passes you going uphill.
Anon

I finally concluded that all failure was from a wobbling will rather than a wobbling wheel.
Frances E. Willard (1839 – 98)

I loathe people who keep dogs. They are cowards who haven't got the guts to bite people themselves.
August Strindberg (1849 – 1912)

To ride a bicycle properly is very much like a love affair; chiefly it is a matter of faith. Believe you can do it and the thing is done; doubt, and for the life of you, you cannot.
H.G. Wells (1866 – 1946)

Every time you are caught behind a huge, fifty-man pile-up there was a strange, putrid odor. It took me years to figure it out: It's the smell of burning flesh.
Bob Roll (1960 -)

I love riding with women. There's no snot blowing, spitting, or dirty jokes. Well I guess there is, but it's more fun when you're the one doing it!!
Anon

Work to eat. Eat to live. Live to bike. Bike to work.
Anon

Ned Flanders: "You were bicycling two abreast?"
Homer Simpson: "I wish".
Dan Castellaneta (1957 -)

The bicycle is a curious vehicle. Its passenger is its engine.
John Howard

Riding a bicycle makes you impotent. That's why I carry a bicycle seat in my pocket—because it's better than wearing a condom.
Jarod Kintz (1982 -)

Socialism can only arrive by bicycle.
Jose Antonio Viera Gallo (1943 -)

Crashing is part of cycling as crying is part of love.
Johan Museeuw (1965 -)

Bones Heal,
Chicks Dig Scars,
Pain is Temporary,
Glory is Forever.
Patrick Aanstoots

There are two types of road bikers: Bikers who are faster than me, and me.
Bruce Cameron (1960 -)

I hope than when I die, my wife sells my bikes for what they are actually worth, not what I told her they cost.
Anon

Go as far as you can see. When you get there, you'll be able to see farther.
JP Morgan (1837 – 1913)

I suppose that was what attracted me to the bicycle right from the start. It is not so much a way of getting somewhere as it is a setting for randomness; it makes every journey an unorganized tour.
Daniel Behrman (1923 – 90)

If you get it wrong, you've got to eat it.
Anon

Chapter 12: DANCING

Dancing is a perpendicular expression of a horizontal desire.
George Bernard Shaw (1856 – 1950)

If dancing were any easier it would be called football.
Anon

I do everything the man does, only backwards and in high heels!
Ginger Rogers (1911- 95)

Almost nobody dances sober, unless they are insane.
HP Lovecraft (1890 – 1937)

**Dancing is the art of getting your feet out of the way
faster than your partner can step on them.**
Anon

**There are only two places where indiscriminate hugging
is tolerated; the brothel and the ballroom.**
M.A. Ham

**If God had intended us to do Ballroom dancing, he would have
made women's knees bend the other way.**
Anon

**Baptists never make love standing up. They're afraid someone
might see them and think they're dancing.**
Lewis Grizzard (1946 – 94)

**My mom took up belly dancing. In order to make it seem like she
was moving, my father and I had to jiggle the furniture in back of
her.**
Rita Rudner (1953 -)

You should make a point of trying every experience once, excepting incest and folk-dancing.
Arnold Bax (1883 – 1953)

I was a ballerina. I had to quit after I injured a groin muscle. It wasn't mine.
Rita Rudner (1953 -)

Ballet: Men wearing pants so tight that you can tell what religion they are.
Robin Williams (1951 – 2014)

Without music, life would be a mistake.... I would only believe in a God who knew how to dance.
Friedrich Nietzsche (1844 – 1900)

In life as in dance: Grace glides on blistered feet.
Alice Abrams

I wish I could shimmy like my sister Kate,
She shivers like jelly on a plate.
Armand J Piron (1888 – 1943)

I could dance with you till the cows come home. On second thoughts, I would rather dance with the cows till you came home.
Groucho Marx (1890 – 1977)

CHAPTER 13: DARTS

Sid Waddell (1940 – 2012)

When Alexander of Macedonia was 33, he cried salt tears because there were no more worlds to conquer ... Bristow's only 27.

It's like trying to pin down a kangaroo on a trampoline.

Steve Beaton - The Adonis of darts, what poise, what elegance - a true roman gladiator with plenty of hair wax.

Jockey Wilson...What an athlete!

He's twitching more than a one legged ferret!

He's got one foot in the frying pan and one on thin ice.

This game of darts is twisting like a rattlesnake with a hernia!

This lad has more checkouts than Tescos.

He looks about as happy as a penguin in a microwave.

Keith Deller is like Long John Silver - he's badly in need of another leg.

Bristow reasons . . . Bristow quickens ... Aaah, Bristow.

Big Cliff Lazarenko's idea of exercise is sitting in a room with the windows open taking the lid off something cool and fizzy.

It's the nearest thing to public execution this side of Saudi Arabia.

That's the greatest comeback since Lazarus.

John Lowe is striding out like Alexander the Great conquering the Persians.

You couldn't get more excitement here if Elvis Presley walked in eating a chip sandwich!

There's no one quicker than these two tungsten tossers.

Bob Anderson ... looking like Lee van Cleef on a bad night!

That's quality with a capital K.

Even Hypotenuse would have trouble working out these angles.

Circus Tavern packed — even a garter snake smothered in Vaseline couldn't slide in here.

Cliff Lazarenko's idea of exercise is a firm press on a soda siphon.

The atmosphere is so tense, if Elvis walked in, with a portion of chips...you could hear the vinegar sizzle on them

His face is sagging with tension.

He is as slick as minestrone soup.

There hasn't been this much excitement since the Romans fed the Christians to the Lions.

The players are under so much duress, it's like duressic park out there!

He's as cool as a prized marrow!

The atmosphere is a cross between the Munich Beer Festival and the Coliseum when the Christians were on the menu.

Trying to read Reyes's mind is like trying to read the mind of Jabba the Hutt.

He's as twitchy as a frog in a blender.

He's like Jack The Ripper on a Friday night.

He's about as predictable as a wasp on speed.

Well as giraffes say, you don't get no leaves unless you stick your neck out.

His eyes are bulging like the belly of a hungry chaffinch.

Eat your heart out Harold Pinter, we've got drama with a capital D in Essex.

He's like D'Artagnan at the scissor factory.

Eyes like a pterodactyl ...with contact lenses.

He's got three legs under his belt and he's running away with the match!

Even the crumpet knows that's not good enough.

He's playing out of his pie crust.

As they say at the DHSS, we're getting the full benefit here.

If we'd had Phil Taylor at Hastings against the Normans, they'd have gone home.

He looks as happy as a scorpion who's just had a pedicure!

This is the clash that makes King Kong versus Godzilla look like a chimpanzees' tea party!

There's only one word for that - magic darts!

They're showing Shakespeare's Othello over on BBC1 but if you want real drama tonight, get down here to Jollies, Stoke-on-Trent.

That could have landed on the pupil of a fly's eyeball

Chapter 14: Fencing

Strange women lying in ponds distributing swords is no basis for a system of government!
Monty Python and the Holy Grail

Those prancing little pants-wetters come here to learn the colorful and gentlemanly art of fencing, with its many sporting limitations and its proscriptions against dishonorable engagements. You on the other hand, you are going to learn how to kill men with a sword.
Scott Lynch (1978 -)

Nothing in life is fair except a witnessed duel.
Lynda Williams (1958-)

Fencing Student: You never taught me that!
Maestro: You can't teach surprise.
Alexander Villard film, 'By The Sword' (1991)

The entire secret of arms consists of only two things: to give, and not to receive.
Moliere (1622 - 1673)

Foil fencers talk about the techniques of fencing. Épée fencers talk about the esoterics of fencing. Sabre fencers talk about themselves.
Nick Evangelista

The French duel is the most health-giving of recreations because of the open-air exercise it affords.
Mark Twain (1835 - 1910)

The sword is one of the few implements that can penetrate both the imagination of man, and his vital organs.
University of Calgary

He who lives by the sword, will eventually be wiped out by some bastard with a sawn off shotgun.
Christopher Widdows (1968 -)

There has been opposition to every innovation in the history of man, with the possible exception of the sword.
Benjamin Dana (1659 - 1738)

The pen is mightier than the sword, until it runs out of ink.
Anon

CHAPTER 15: FISHING

Fishing is a delusion entirely surrounded by liars in old clothes.
Don Marquis (1878 - 1937)

There are worse things in life than death. Have you ever spent an evening with a fisherman?
Woody Allen (1935 -)

Old fishermen never die, they just smell that way
Anon

I fell in love with a fly fisherman... I can't believe my competition is a fish, and not other women.
Allison Moir (1966 -)

There's a fine line between fishing and just standing on the shore like an idiot.
Steven Wright (1955 -)

It has always been my private conviction that any man who pits his intelligence against a fish and loses has it coming.
John Steinbeck (1902 - 1968)

The formal term for a collection of fishermen is an exaggeration.
Anon

All the romance of trout fishing exists in the mind of the angler and is in no way shared by the fish.
Harold F. Blaisdell (1901 - 1971)

All fishermen are liars; it's an occupational disease with them like housemaid's knee or editor's ulcers.
Beatrice Cook

Fishing is boring, unless you catch an actual fish, and then it is disgusting.
Dave Barry (1947 -)

There is no greater fan of fly fishing than the worm.
Patrick F. McManus (1932 -)

If fishing is a religion, fly fishing is high church.
Tom Brokaw (1940 -)

The fish and I were both stunned and disbelieving to find ourselves connected by a line.
William Humphrey (1967 -)

Guests, like fish, begin to smell after three days.
Benjamin Franklin (1706 - 1790)

Nothing grows faster than a fish from when it bites until it gets away.
Anon

Even a fish wouldn't get into trouble if it kept its mouth shut.
Anon

My biggest worry is that my wife (when I'm dead) will sell my fishing gear for what I said I paid for it.
Koos Brandt

A fishing rod is a stick with a hook at one end and a fool at the other.
Samuel Johnson (1709 - 1784)

Surely the best virtue of fishermen is their hopefulness.
Zane Grey (1872 -1939)

Anglers exaggerate grossly and make gentle and inoffensive creatures sound like wounded buffalo and wounded man-eating tigers.
Roderick Haig-Brown (1908 - 1979)

The difference between fly fishers and worm dunkers is the quality of their excuses.
Anon

All Americans believe that they are born fishermen. For a man to admit a distaste for fishing would be like denouncing mother-love or hating moonlight.
John Steinbeck (1902 - 1968)

Even if you've been fishing for 3 hours and haven't gotten anything except poison ivy and sunburn, you're still better off than the worm
Anon

The best way to a fisherman's heart is through his fly.
Anon

Fishing...is a discipline in the equality of men – for all men are equal before the fish.
Herbert Hoover (1874 - 1964)

Fly fishing is like sex: everyone thinks there is more than there is, and everyone is getting more than their fair share.
Henry Kanemoto

Fishing is the sport of drowning worms.
Anon

The fishing was good; it was the catching that was bad.
A.K. Best

I never drink water because of the disgusting things that fish do in it.
W. C. Fields (1880 – 1946)

There he stands, draped in more equipment than a telephone lineman, trying to outwit an organism with a brain no bigger than a breadcrumb, and getting licked in the process.
Paul O'Neil

Bragging may not bring happiness, but no man having caught a large fish goes home through an alley.
Ann Landers (1918 - 2002)

Anglers think they are diving some primeval natural force by outwitting a fish, a creature that never even got out of the evolutionary starting gate.
Rich Hall (1954 -)

Fishing is a jerk on one end of the line waiting, for a jerk on the other end of the line
Anon

The only reason I ever played golf in the first place was so that I could afford to hunt and fish.
Sam Snead (1912 - 2002)

The solution to any problem -- work, love, money, whatever -- is to go fishing, and the worse the problem, the longer the trip should be.
John Gierach (1946 -)

There's a reason they call it fishing and not catching.
Anon

Catch and Release fishing is a lot like golf. You don't have to eat the ball to have a good time.
Anon

In fishing and in life, the problem with common sense is that it's not all that common.
Lefty Kreh (1926 -)

No human being, however great, or powerful, was ever so free as a fish.
John Ruskin (1819 - 1900)

Give a man a fish, and you'll feed him for a day; give him a religion, and he'll starve to death while praying for a fish.
Anon

Fishermen and hypochondriacs have one thing in common – they don't have to catch anything to be happy.
Robert Orben (1927 -)

I love fishing. It's like transcendental meditation with a punchline.
Billy Connolly (1942 -)

It is not a fish until it is on the bank.
Irish Proverb

CHAPTER 16: GOLF

Hockey is a sport for white men. Basketball is a sport for black men. Golf is a sport for white men dressed like black pimps.
Tiger Woods (1975 -)

Golf is essentially an exercise in masochism conducted out-of-doors.
Paul O'Neil (1963 -)

I am very lucky. If it wasn't for golf I don't know what I would have done. If my IQ had been two points lower, I'd have been a plant somewhere.
Lee Trevino (1939 -)

Why am I using a new putter? Because the last one didn't float too well.
Craig Stadler (1953 -)

The difference between golf and government is that in golf you can't improve your lie.
George Deukmejian (1928 -)

The best wood in most amateurs' bags is the pencil.
Anon

Isn't it fun to go out on the course and lie in the sun?
Bob Hope (1903 – 2003)

Golf is an ineffectual attempt to put an elusive ball into an obscure hole with implements ill-adapted to the purpose.
Woodrow Wilson (1856 - 1924)

While playing golf today I hit two good balls. I stepped on a rake.
Henry Youngman (1906 – 98)

Golf and sex are about the only things you can enjoy without being good at.
Jimmy Demaret (1910 – 83)

I'd like to see the fairways more narrow. Then everybody would have to play from the rough, not just me
Seve Ballesteros (1957 – 2011)

I never exaggerate. I just remember big.
Chi Chi Rodriguez (1935 -)

I would like to deny all allegations by Bob Hope that during my last game of golf, I hit an eagle, a birdie, an elk and a moose.
Gerald Ford (1913 – 2006)

You can make a lot of money in this game. Just ask my ex -wives. Both of them are so rich that neither of their husbands works.
Lee Trevino (1939 -)

The only sure rule in golf is he who has the fastest cart never has to play the bad lie.
Mickey Mantle (1931 - 1995)

Golf... is the infallible test. The man who can go into a patch of rough alone, with the knowledge that only God is watching him, and play his ball where it lies, is the man who will serve you faithfully and well.
P.G. Wodehouse (1881 – 1975)

If profanity had an influence on the flight of the ball, the game of golf would be played far better than it is.
Horace G. Hutchinson (1859-1932)

On a recent survey, 80% of golfers admitted cheating. The other 20% lied.
Bruce Lansky (1941 -)

I've spent most of my life golfing — the rest I've just wasted.
Anon

The reason a pro tells you to keep your head down is so you can't see him laughing.
Phyllis Diller (1917 - 2012)

If you're caught on a golf course during a storm and are afraid of lightning, hold up a 1-iron. Not even God can hit a 1-iron.
Lee Trevino (1939 -)

We learn many things from gold. How to suffer for example.
Bruce Lansky (1941 -)

I know I am getting better at golf because I am hitting fewer spectators.
Gerald R. Ford (1913 - 2006)

I like golf because you can be really terrible at it and still not look much dorkier than anyone else.
Dave Barry (1947 -)

I have a tip that can take five strokes off anyone's game: It's called an eraser.
Arnold Palmer (1929 -)

I call upon all nations to do everything they can to stop these terrorist killers. Thank you. Now watch this drive.
George W. Bush (1946 -)

I regard golf as an expensive way of playing marbles.
G.K. Chesterton (1874 - 1936)

As you walk down the fairway of life, you must smell the roses, for you only get to play one round.
Ben Hogan (1912 - 1997)

Give me golf clubs, fresh air and a beautiful partner, and you can keep the clubs and the fresh air.
Jack Benny (1894 - 1974)

Golf is a lot of walking, broken up by disappointment and bad arithmetic

Anon

Golf is a fascinating game. It has taken me nearly forty years to discover that I can't play it.

Ted Ray(1905-1977)

We learn so many things from golf—how to suffer, for instance.

Bruce Lansky (1941 -)

Although golf was originally restricted to wealthy, overweight Protestants, today it's open to anybody who owns hideous clothing.

Dave Barry (1947 -)

The least thing upset him on the links. He missed short putts because of the uproar of butterflies in the adjoining meadows.

P.G. Wodehouse (1881 – 1975)

The number of shots taken by an opponent who is out of sight is equal to the square root of the sum of the number of curses heard plus the number of swishes.

Michael Green (1946 -)

Golf is a day spent in a round of strenuous idleness.

William Wordsworth (1770 - 1850)

Is my friend in the bunker or is the bastard on the green?

David Feherty (1958 -)

Man blames fate for other accidents but feels personally responsible for a hole in one.

Martha Beckman

My swing is so bad I look like a caveman killing his lunch.

Lee Trevino (1939 -)

Golf is the cruelest of sports. Like life, it's unfair. It's a harlot. A trollop. It leads you on. It never lives up to its promises.... It's a boulevard of broken dreams. It plays with men. And runs off with the butcher.
Jim Murray (1957 -)

Golf is an open exhibition of overweening ambition, courage deflated by stupidity, skill scoured by a whiff of arrogance.
Alistair Cooke (1908 - 2004)

Golf is a game in which you yell "fore," shoot six, and write down five.
Paul Harvey (1918 - 2009)

These greens are so fast I have to hold my putter over the ball and hit it with the shadow.
Sam Snead (1912 - 2002)

A "gimme" can best be defined as an agreement between two golfers, neither of whom can putt very well.
Anon

Art said he wanted to get more distance. I told him to hit it and run backward.
Ken Venturi (1931 - 2013)

The only time my prayers are never answered is on the golf course.
Billy Graham (1918 -)

To some golfers, the greatest handicap is the ability to add correctly.
Anon

Golf can best be defined as an endless series of tragedies obscured by the occasional miracle.
Anon

My favorite shots are the practice swing and the conceded putt. The rest can never be mastered.
Lord Robertson (1946 -)

Golf is a good walk spoiled.
Mark Twain (1835 – 1910)

CHAPTER 17: GYMNASTICS

In Russia, show the least athletic aptitude and they have got you dangling off the parallel bars with a leotard full of hormones.
Victoria Wood (1953 -)

Rhythmic gymnastics: adolescent girls the size of pixies, made up like the women on department store perfume counters, grinning like corpses while they wave a ribbon or bounce a ball.
The Guardian

After a day of football, a gymnast would be bruised. After a day of gymnastics, a footballer would be dead.
Anon

If gymnastics were easy it would be called cheerleading.
Anon

Life is like gymnastics. It's better if you're flexible
Anon

Soccer players use shin guards to protect them. Volleyball players use knee pads to protect them. Football players use shoulder pads, helmets and numerous other pads to protect them. Gymnasts use nothing but their pride.
Anon

All the power of a linebacker in a much prettier package.
Anon

CHAPTER 18: HORSE RACING

A difference of opinion is what makes horse racing and missionaries.
Will Rogers (1879 – 1935)

Horse sense is the thing a horse has which keeps it from betting on people.
W.C. Fields (1880 -1946)

A bookie is just a pickpocket who lets you use your own hands.
Henry Morgan (1635 – 1688)

You could remove the brains from 90% of jockeys and they would weigh the same.
John Francome (1952 -)

Luck never gives; it only lends.
Swedish Proverb

A racehorse is an animal that can take several thousand people for a ride at the same time.
Anon

I am not one of the people who believe that the main reason why a chap becomes a bookmaker is because he is too scared to steal and too heavy to become a jockey.
Noel Whitcombe (1918 – 93)

The horse I bet on had four legs and flies - unfortunately it was a dead horse
Anon

Owning a racehorse is probably the most expensive way of getting on to a racecourse for nothing.
Clement Freud (1924 – 2009)

What a pity people don't take as much trouble with their own breeding as intelligent racehorse owners do. But then I suppose it is bordering on fascism to think like that.
Jeffrey Barnard (1932 – 97)

I see no particular objection to giving women a chance to ride in races now and again ... such races should be on the Flat and be placed last on the card so that those racegoers not interested can return home for tea and Magic Roundabout.
Roger Mortimer (1909 -91)

If Jesus Christ rode his flaming donkey like you just rode that horse, then he deserved to be crucified.
Fred Rimell (1913 – 81)

A good jockey doesn't need orders and a bad jockey couldn't carry them out anyway; so it's best not to give them any.
Lester Piggott (1935 -)

I'm lucky because I have an athlete between my legs.
Willie Carson (1942 -)

There are, they say, fools, bloody fools and men who remount in a steeplechase.
John Oaksey (1929 – 2012)

A real racehorse should have a head like a lady and the behind like a cook.
Jack Leach

Lochsong - she's like Linford Christie ... without the lunchbox.
Frankie Dettori (1970 -)

Eventually the pool from which stewards were selected was extended beyond the registered blind, the chronically inbred and those whose ear trumpets or searing gout problems rendered them half-sharp or pathologically vicious.
Alastair Down

With some justification the Jockey Club has been described as 'the purest example of the 18th century to survive in Britain'.
John Purvis

There are three racecourses beginning with the letter F - namely Fontwell, Folkestone and effing Plumpton.
Fred Winter (1926 – 2004)

This is really a lovely horse; I once rode her mother.
Ted Walsh (1950 -)

Love is... paying a £500 vet bill for a horse worth £50.
Anon

Other than being castrated, things have gone quite well for Funny Cide.
Kenny Mayne (1959 -)

In a bet there is a fool and a thief.
Proverb

Horse racing is animated roulette.
Roger Kahn (1927 -)

Why did I become a jockey? I was too small to become a window cleaner and too big to be a garden gnome.
Adrian McGuire (1971 -)

It's hard to lead a cavalry charge if you think you look funny on a horse.
Adlai E. Stevenson (1930 -)

But what truly horsey girls discover in the end is that boyfriends, husbands, children, and careers are the substitute-for horses.
Jane Smiley (1949 -)

A horse which stops dead just before a jump and thus propels its rider into a graceful arc provides a splendid excuse for general merriment.
H.R.H. Prince Philip (1921 -)

I bet on a horse the other day that was so slow the jockey kept a diary of the trip.
Bob Monkhouse (1928 – 2003)

A gambler is nothing but a man who makes his living out of hope.
William Bolitho (1890 – 1930)

In most betting shops you will see three windows marked 'Bet Here', but only one window with the legend 'Pay Out'.
Jeffrey Barnard (1932 – 97)

No one has ever bet enough on a winning horse.
Richard Sasuly

The only exercise I get is walking to the betting office.
Peter O'Sullevan (1918 – 2015)

The only tip I can give on jumpers is -where to buy them in London.
Henry Cecil (1943 – 2013)

I have stood in a bar in Lambourn and been offered, in the space of five minutes, a poached salmon, a leg of a horse, a free trip to Chantilly, marriage, a large unsolicited loan, ten tips for a ten-horse race, two second-hand cars, a fight, and the copyright to a dying jockey's life story.
Jeffrey Barnard (1932 – 97)

On a horse that consistently hung left-The best thing you can do is put a bit of lead in his right ear, to act as a counterbalance ... with a shotgun.
Lester Piggott (1935 -)

Mother always told me my day was coming, but I never realised I'd end up being the shortest knight of the year.
Sir Gordon Richards (1904 – 86)

If a horse is no good, trade him for a dog, then shoot the dog.
Ben Jones (1882 – 1961)

If you could call the thing a horse. If it hadn't shown a flash of speed in the straight, it would have got mixed up with the next race.
P. G. Wodehouse (1881 – 1975)

When I hear somebody talk about a horse or cow being stupid; I figure it's a sure sign that the animal has somehow outfoxed them.
Tom Dorrance (1910 – 2003)

In betting on races, there are two elements that are never lacking - hope as hope, and an incomplete recollection of the past.
Edward V. Lucas (1868 – 1938)

If you want to understand the effect of weight on a horse, try running for a bus with nothing in your hands. Then try doing it with your hands full of shopping. Then think about doing that for four and a half miles.
Jenny Pitman (1946 -)

I was young and fearless in those days, but always enjoyed riding at Cartmel. They used to call me 'Cartmellor', probably because I kept coming back on a stretcher.
Stan Mellor (1937 -)

There is only one race greater than the Jews - and that is the Derby.
Victor Sassoon (1881 – 1961)

Money won is twice as sweet as money earned.
Eddie Felson (The Color of Money) 1986

You need luck as well as good blood lines to produce a horse like Secretariat. It's a funny thing. For instance, Secretariat has a half-sister who looks like a potential winner. But he also has a half-sister who couldn't outrun a fat man going downhill.
Helen Tweedy (1922 -

Someone suggested that the Jockey Club Race Planning Committee consisted of a table and four chairs - and I bet they've got woodworm.
Jenny Pitman (1946 -)

Stewards are, on the whole, simple folk. Most them come from a social class in which inbreeding has taken its toll.
Paul Haigh

There are only two emotions that belong in the saddle; one is a sense of humor and the other is patience.
John Lyons

Equestrian activity teaches young ladies to cope with large, friendly, but dumb creatures – the ideal training for marriage.
Anon

A profit at the race track isn't a profit until you spend it somewhere else.
Charles Carroll

The race is not always to the swift, or the battle to the strong, but that is the way to bet.
Damon Runyon (1880 – 1946)

I backed a great horse the other day. It took eight horses to beat him.
Henry Youngman (1906 – 98)

Dear Lord, help me to break even. I need the money.
Anon

CHAPTER 19: HUNTING

I ask people why they have deer heads on their walls. They always say because it's such a beautiful animal. There you go. I think my mother is attractive, but I have photographs of her.
Ellen DeGeneres (1958 -)

The fascination of shooting as a sport depends almost wholly on whether you are at the right or wrong end of the gun.
P.G. Wodehouse (1881 – 1975)

The search for a scapegoat is the easiest of all hunting expeditions.
Dwight D. Eisenhower (1890 – 1965)

Going to war without France is like going hunting without an accordion.
Norman Schwarzkopf (1934 – 2012)

The perils of duck hunting are great - especially for the duck.
Walter Cronkite (1916 – 2009)

I love things made out of animals. It's just so funny to think of someone saying, 'I need a letter opener. I guess I'll have to kill a deer'.
David Sedaris (1956 -)

You have to pay for every bird you kill and the coin you use to pay for them is time.
Tom Kelly

Until lions have their historians, tales of the hunt shall always glorify the hunter"
African Proverb

People never lie so much as after a hunt, during a war or before an election.
Otto von Bismarck (1815 – 98)

Before beginning a Hunt, it is wise to ask someone what you are looking for before you begin looking for it.
Winnie the Pooh

Don't think to hunt two hares with one dog.
Benjamin Franklin (1706 – 90)

If you turn the imagination loose like a hunting dog, it will often return with the bird in its mouth.
William Maxwell (1908 – 2000)

A bird was shot. I suspect fowl play. The next man to be shot is the man who wrote that pun. Excuse me while I load my gun and shoot myself.
Jarod Kintz (1982 -)

When a man wants to murder a tiger he calls it sport; when a tiger wants to murder him he calls it ferocity."
George Bernard Shaw (1856 – 1950)

One knows so well the popular idea of health. The English country gentleman galloping after a fox - the unspeakable in full pursuit of the uneatable.
Oscar Wilde (1854 – 1900)

Whenever I see a photograph of some sportsman grinning over his kill, I am always impressed by the striking moral and esthetic superiority of the dead animal to the live one.
Edward Abbey (1927 – 89)

If God didn't want men to hunt, he wouldn't have given him plaid shirts.
Johnny Carson (1925 – 2005)

I don't see why I should break a neck because a dog chooses to run after a nasty smell
Arthur Balfour (1848 – 1930)

CHAPTER 20: ICE HOCKEY

I went to a fight the other night and a hockey game broke out.
Rodney Dangerfield (1921 – 2004)

Playing 'Send in the Clowns' when the referee and officials went on the ice was inappropriate, and was further compounded when he played 'three blind mice' when they left.
Nottingham Panthers Official

If you've got one day to live, come to see the Toronto Maple Leafs play. It will seem like forever.
Pat Foley (1954 -)

By the age of 18, the average American has witnessed 200,000 acts of violence on television, most of them occurring during Game 1 of the NHL playoff series.
Steve Rushin (1966 -)

Four out of five dentists surveyed recommended playing hockey.
Anon

They say you're not a coach in the league till you've been fired. I must be getting pretty good.
Terry Simpson (1943 -)

Goaltending is a normal job, sure. How would you like it in your job if every time you made a small mistake, a red light went on over your desk and 15,000 people stood up and yelled at you?
Jacques Plante (1929 – 86)

The only way you can check Gretzky is to hit him when he is standing still singing the national anthem.
Harry Sinden (1932 -)

Half the game is mental; the other half is being mental.
Jim McKenny (1946 -)

Hockey players wear numbers because you can't always identify the body with dental records.
Bob Plager (1943 -)

High sticking, tripping, slashing, spearing, charging, hooking, fighting, unsportsmanlike conduct, interference, roughing......everything else is just figure skating.
Scott Bowman (1933 -)

Hockey belongs to the Cartoon Network, where a person can be pancaked by an ACME anvil, then expanded - accordion-style - back to full stature, without any lasting side effect.
Steve Rushin (1966 -)

Hockey is figure skating in a war zone.
Anon

Red ice sells hockey tickets.
Bob Stewart (1950 -)

Some guys play hockey. Gretzky plays 40 mph chess.
Lowell Cohn

You miss 100% of the shots you never take.
Wayne Gretzky (1961 -)

I was a multi-millionaire from playing hockey. Then I got divorced, and now I am a millionaire.
Bobby Hull. (1939 -)

You're playing worse every day and right now you're playing like the middle of next week.
Herb Brooks (1937 – 2003)

The only difference between this and Custer's last stand was Custer didn't have to look at the tape afterwards.
Terry Crisp (1943 -)

Goaltenders are three sandwiches shy of a picnic. From the moment primitive man lurched erect, he survived on the principle that when something hard and potentially lethal comes toward you at great velocity, get the hell out of its path.
Jim Taylor

The three important elements of hockey are: forecheck, backcheck and paycheck.
Gil Perreault (1950 -)

Ice hockey is a form of disorderly conduct in which the score is kept.
Doug Larson (1926 -)

A puck is a hard rubber disc that hockey players strike when they can't hit one another.
Jimmy Cannon (1909 – 73)

We get nose jobs all the time in the NHL, and we don't even have to go to the hospital.
Brad Park (1948 -)

Street hockey is great for kids. It's energetic, competitive, and skillful. And best of all, it keeps them off the street.
Gus Kyle (1923 – 96)

I love those hockey moms. You know the difference between a hockey mom and a pit bull? Lipstick.
Sarah Palin (1964 -)

Chapter 21: Motor Racing

Racing is the best way of converting money into noise.
Anon

Driving fast on the track doesn't scare me. What scares me is when I am driving on the highway and get overtaken by some idiot who thinks he is Fangio
Juan Fangio (1911 – 95)

Racing makes heroin addiction look like a vague wish for something salty.
Peter Egan (1946 -)

Simplify; then add lightness.
Colin Chapman (1928 – 82)

Tonight, the new Viper, which is the American equivalent of a sports car... in the same way, I guess, that George Bush is the equivalent of a President.
Jeremy Clarkson (1960 -)

Straight roads are for fast cars. Turns are for fast drivers.
Colin McRae (1968 – 2007)

Aerodynamics are for people who can't build cars.
Enzo Ferrari (1898 – 1988)

Newman's First Law; It is useless to put your brakes on if your car is upside down.
Paul Newman (1925 – 2008)

Cheap, fast and reliable. Pick two.
Anon

If everything seems under control your just not going fast enough.
Mario Andretti (1940 -)

In the olden days I always got the impression that TVR built a car, put it on sale, and then found out how it handled. Usually when one of their customers wrote to the factory complaining about how dead he was.
Jeremy Clarkson (1960 -)

He who turns least wins.
Ross Bentley (1962 -)

Second place is just the first place loser.
Dale Earnhardt (1951 – 2001)

Better to be a racer for a moment than a spectator for a lifetime.
Anon

Oversteer scares passengers; understeer scares drivers.
Anon

The Ferrari 355 is like a quail's egg dipped in celery salt and served in Julia Roberts' belly button.
Jeremy Clarkson (1960 -)

Auto racing, bull fighting, and mountain climbing are the only real sports... all others are just games.
Ernest Hemingway (1899 – 1961)

You know, race car driving is like sex. All men think they are good at it.
Jay Leno (1950 -)

A crazy man finishes in the cemetery.
Juan Fangio (1911 – 95)

Everyone behind me is an incredibly talented driver - Everyone in front of me is cheating!
Bill Haney

You win some, lose some, and wreck some.
Dale Earnhardt (1951 – 2001)

The lead car is absolutely unique, except for the one behind it which is identical.
Murray Walker (1923 -)

Speed has never killed anyone, suddenly becoming stationary... that's what gets you.
Jeremy Clarkson (1960 -)

You can't fix stupid.
Larry Morgan

Aston Martin DB9... that's not really a racing car, that's just pornography.
Jeremy Clarkson (1960 -)

After the third flip, I lost control...
Don Roberts

When I raced a car last it was at a time when sex was safe and racing was dangerous. Now, it's the other way round.
Hans Stuck (1951 -)

Winning is everything. The only ones who remember you when you come second are your wife and your dog.
Damon Hill (1960 -)

I drive way too fast to worry about cholesterol.
Steven Wright (1955 -)

Telling people at a dinner party you drive a Nissan Almera is like telling them you've got the ebola virus and you're about to sneeze.
Jeremy Clarkson (1960 -)

Mansell knows where he is because he can see him in his earphones.
Murray Walker (1923 -)

Motor racing's less of a sport these days than a commercial break doing 150 mph.
Peter Dunne

I don't make mistakes; I make prophecies that immediately turn out to be wrong
Murray Walker (1923 -)

There's nothing wrong with the car except that it's on fire.
Murray Walker (1923 -)

And now, excuse me while I interrupt myself.
Murray Walker (1923 -)

The lead car is unique, except for the one behind it which is identical.
Murray Walker (1923 -)

Murray Walker is a man who even in rare moments of tranquility sounds like his trousers are on fire!
Clive James (1939 -)

CHAPTER 22: RUGBY

The relationship between the Welsh and the English is based on trust and understanding. They don't trust us and we don't understand them.
Dudley Wood (1930 -)

The first half is invariably much longer than the second. This is partly because of the late kick-off but is also caused by the unfitness of the referee.
Michael Green (1946 -)

A major rugby tour by the British Isles to New Zealand is a cross between a medieval crusade and a prep school outing.
John Hopkins

Look what these bastards have done to Wales. They've taken our coal, our water, our steel. They buy our houses and they only live in them for a fortnight every 12 months. What have they given us? Absolutely nothing. We've been exploited, raped, controlled and punished by the English - and that's who you are playing this afternoon.
Phil Bennett (1948 -)

England's coach Jack Powell, an immensely successful businessman, has the acerbic wit of Dorothy Parker and, according to most New Zealanders, a similar knowledge of rugby.
Mark Reason

Rugby is played by men with odd shaped balls.
Anon

The women sit, getting colder and colder, on a seat getting harder and harder, watching oafs, getting muddier and muddier.
Virginia Graham (1912 - 1998)

If we have to play against New Zealand, I'll explain it like this. To win, their 15 players have to have a diarrhoea and we will have to put snipers around the field shooting at them and then we have to play the best match of our lives.
Juan Martin Fernandez Lobbe (1981 -)

I'd like to thank the press from the heart of my bottom.
Nick Easter (1978 -)

The advantage law is the best law in rugby, because it lets you ignore all the others for the good of the game.
Derek Robinson (1932 -)

I think you enjoy the game more if you don't know the rules. Anyway, you're on the same wavelength as the referees.
Jonathan Davies (1962 -)

I prefer rugby to soccer. I enjoy the violence in rugby, except when they start biting each other's ears off.
Elizabeth Taylor (1932 - 2011)

Rugby is a good occasion for keeping thirty bullies far from the center of the city.
Oscar Wilde (1854 - 1900)

I think Brian Moore's gnashers are the kind you get from a DIY shop and hammer in yourself. He is the only player we have who looks like a French forward.
Paul Randall (1958 -)

If the game is run properly as a professional game, you do not need 57 old farts running rugby.
Will Carling (1965 -)

Rugby is a game for big buggers. if you're not a big bugger, you get hurt. I wasn't a big bugger but i was a fast bugger and therefore I avoided the big buggers.
Spike Milligan (1918 - 2002)

Ballroom dancing is a contact sport. Rugby is a collision sport.
Heyneke Meyer (1967 -)

The Holy Writ of Gloucester Rugby Club demands: first, that the forwards shall win the ball; second, that the forwards shall keep the ball; and third, the backs shall buy the beer.
Doug Ibbotson

Nobody in Rugby should be called a genius. A genius is a guy like Norman Einstein.
Jono Gibbs (1977 -)

He scored that try after only 22 seconds - totally against the run of play.
Murray Mexted (1953 -)

Remember that rugby is a team game; all 14 of you make sure you pass the ball to Jonah.
Anon fax to N.Z. team

No leadership, no ideas. Not even enough imagination to thump someone in the line-up when the ref wasn't looking.
J.P.R. Williams (1949 -)

I don't know about us not having a Plan B when things went wrong, we looked like we didn't have a Plan A.
Geoff Cooke (1941 -)

In my time, I've had my knee out, broken my collarbone, had my nose smashed, a rib broken, lost a few teeth, and ricked my back; but as soon as I get a bit of bad luck I'm going to quit the game.
J. W. Robinson (1974 -)

A forward's usefulness to his side varies as to the square of his distance from the ball.
Clarrie Gibbons

Forwards are the gnarled and scarred creatures who have a propensity for running into and bleeding all over each other.
Peter Fitzsimmons (1961 -)

I never comment on referees and I'm not going to break the habit of a lifetime for that prat.
Ewan McKenzice. (1965 -)

Rugby backs can be identified because they generally have clean jerseys and identifiable partings in their hair... come the revolution the backs will be the first to be lined up against the wall and shot for living parasitically off the work of others.
Peter Fizsimmons (1961 -)

Rugby is a game for the mentally deficient... That is why it was invented by the British. Who else but an Englishman could invent an oval ball?
Peter Pook (1918 - 1978)

The tactical difference between Association Football and Rugby with its varieties seems to be that in the former, the ball is he missile, in the latter, men are the missles. *Alfred E. Crawley (1869 - 1924)*

CHAPTER 23: SAILING

The lovely thing about cruising is that planning usually turns out to be of little use.
Dom Degnon

The chance for mistakes is about equal to the number of crew squared.
Ted Turner (1938 -)

There are three sorts of people; those who are alive, those who are dead, and those who are at sea.
Anacharsis

Ocean racingis like standing in a cold shower in a howling gale tearing up twenty pound notes.
Edward Heath (1916 – 2005)

Only fools and passengers drink at sea.
Allan Villiers (1903 - 1982)

Gentlemen, when the enemy is committed to a mistake we must not interrupt him too soon.
Horatio Nelson (1758 - 1805)

No man will be a sailor who has contrivance enough to get himself into a jail; for being in a ship is being in a jail, with the chance of being drowned. A man in a jail has more room, better food and commonly better company.
Samuel Johnson (1709 - 1784)

The man who's not afraid of the sea'll soon be drowned for he'll go out on a day he shouldn't. But we be afraid of the sea so we only be drowned now and again.
James Clavell "Shogun" (1924 - 1994)

Sailing - The fine art of slowly going nowhere at great expense while being cold, wet and miserable.
Irv Heller

Only two sailors, in my experience, never ran aground. One never left port and the other was an atrocious liar.
Don Bamford

A man can pretend to be a lot of things in this world; but he can only pretend to be a sailor for as long as it takes to clear the harbour mouth!
Bernard Hayman (1930 - 2002)

Sailing, the most expensive way to travel 3rd class.
Anon

A lot of people ask me if I were shipwrecked, and could only have one book, what would it be? I always say 'How to Build a Boat'.
Stephen Wright (1955 -)

Cruising has two pleasures. One is to go out in wider waters from a sheltered place. The other is to go into a sheltered place from wider waters.
Howard Bloomfield

One of the best temporary cures for pride and affection is seasickness.
Henry Wheeler Show

Off Cape Horn there are but two kinds of weather, neither one of them a pleasant kind.
John Masefield (1878 - 1967)

There is but a plank between a sailor and eternity.
Thomas Gibbons (1904 - 1988)

Money can't buy you happiness, but it can buy you a yacht big enough to pull up right alongside it.
Anon

The Americas Cup is a race of management, money, technology, teamwork and, last and incidentally, sailing.
Bill Koch (1940 -)

A ship is always referred to as "she" because it costs so much to keep one in paint and powder.
Chester W. Nimitz (1885 - 1966)

I want a boat that drinks 6, eats 4, and sleeps 2.
Ernest K. Gann (1910 - 1991)

The man who has experienced shipwreck shudders even at a calm sea.
Ovid (43BC - 18AD)

Until you have the courage to lose sight of the shore, you will not know the terror of being forever lost at sea.
Charles Cook

The pessimist complains about the wind; the optimist expects it to change; the realist adjusts the sails. William
Arthur Ward (1921 - 1994)

There is nothing - absolutely nothing - half so much worth doing as simply messing about in boats.
Kenneth Grahame (1859 - 1932)

Attitude is the difference between ordeal and adventure
Bob Bitchin (1944 -)

Wind is to us what money is to life on shore.
Sterling Hayden (1916 - 1986)

Not all who wander are lost.
JRR Tolkien (1892 - 1973)

He that will not sail till all dangers are over must never put to sea.
Thomas Fuller (1608 - 1661)

Red dress in morning, Sailors take warning...
Sterling Hayden (1916 - 1986)

It's scary to have a 30-foot wave chasing you. If you are steering, you don't look back. The crew looks back for you, and you watch their faces. When they look straight up, then get ready!
Magnus Olsson (1949 - 2013)

To the question, "When were your spirits at the lowest ebb?" the obvious answer seemed to be, "When the gin gave out."
Sir Francis Chichester (1901 - 1972)

Should you find yourself in a chronically leaking boat, energy devoted to changing vessels is likely to be more productive than energy devoted to patching leaks.
Warren Buffett (1930 -)

A small craft in an ocean is, or should be, a benevolent dictatorship.
Tristan Jones (1929 - 1995)

When I lost my rifle, the Army charged me 85 dollars. That is why in the Navy the Captain goes down with the ship.
Dick Gregory (1932 -)

Only fools and passengers drink at sea.
Allan Villiers (1903 - 1982)

CHAPTER 24: SKIING

Stretch pants - the garment that made skiing a spectator sport.
Anon

The first time I went skiing I wasn't very good, and broke a leg. Luckily, it wasn't one of mine.
Michael Green (1927 -)

Skiing combines outdoor fun with knocking down trees with your face.
Dave Barry (1949 -)

All things are possible, except for skiing through a revolving door.
Anon

Skis are a pair of long, thin flexible runners that permit a skier to slide across the snow and into debt.
Henry Beard (1945 -)

Snowboarding is an activity that is very popular with people who do not feel that regular skiing is lethal enough.
Dave Barry (1949 -)

I do uphill skiing; I don't do downhill skiing. I think that's for nerd amateurs.
Judah Friedlander (1969 -)

A ski jacket is the larval stage of a blimp.
Henry Beard (1945 -)

There are only four things you can do on skis. Turn right, turn left, go straight, or sell them.
Warren Miller (1924 -)

Skiing? Why break my leg at 40 degrees below when I can fall downstairs at home?
Corey Ford (1902 - 1969)

Skiing is the best way in the world to waste time.
Glen Plake (1964 -)

Luge strategy? Lie flat and try not to die.
Tim Steeves

The luge is what I would callthe ultimate laxative.
Otto Jelinek (1940 -)

Most skiers are really motorcyclists in cute clothes
Bob Wilkerson (1954 -)

You can't get hurt in the air, man!
Anon

There are really only three things to learn in skiing: how to put on your skis, how to slide downhill, and how to walk along the hospital corridor.
Lord Mancroft (1957 -)

When it comes to skiing, there's a difference between what you think it's going to be like, what it's really like, and what you tell your friends it was like.
Anon

Traverse: One of two ways to stop while skiing. Tree: The other method.
Anon

I think my favorite sport in the Olympics is the one in which you make your way through the snow, you stop, you shoot a gun, and then you continue on. In most of the world, it is known as the biathlon, except in New York City, where it is known as winter.
Michael Ventre

I've used up all my sick days, so I called in dead.
Anon

If at first you don't succeed, failure may be your thing.
Warren Miller (1924 -)

The sport of skiing consists of wearing three thousand dollars' worth of clothes and equipment and driving two hundred miles in the snow in order to stand around at a bar and get drunk.
P.J. O'Rourke (1947 -)

Skiing is the only sport where you spend an arm and a leg to break an arm and a leg.
Anon

I do not participate in any sport with ambulances at the bottom of the hill.
Erma Bombeck (1927 - 1996)

The best thing about skiing backwards is you can see where you've been.
Warren Miller (1924 -)

CHAPTER 25: SNOOKER/POOL

Steve is going for the pink ball - and for those of you who are watching in black and white, the pink is next to the green.
Ted Lowe (1920 - 2011)

When I played pool I was like a good psychiatrist. I cured 'em of all their daydreams and delusions.
Minesota Fats

I think it's a great idea to talk during sex, as long as it's about snooker.
Steve Davis (1957 -)

Dressing a pool player in a tuxedo is like putting whipped cream on a hot dog.
Minnesota Fats

That's inches away from being millimeter perfect
Ted Lowe (1920 - 2011)

I suppose the charisma bypass operation was a big disappointment in my life.
Steve Davis (1957 -)

I remember when Steve Davis used to take valium as a stimulant.
Dennis Taylor (1949 -)

Snooker is a game of simple shots played to perfection.
Joe Davies (1901 - 1978)

Somebody said to me theother day that there are no characters left in the game. I asked him who his favorite player was and he said Terry Griffiths. That threw me a bit.
John Virgo (1946 -)

Matthew Stevens' natural expression is that of a man who may have mislaid his winning lottery tcket.
Paul Weaver

Stephen Hendry jumps on Steve Davis' misses every chance he gets.
Mike Hallet (1959 -)

Billiards is very similar to snooker, except there are only three balls and nobody watches it.
Steve Davis (1957 -)

The formalities are now over and it's down to business, Steve Davis now adjusting his socks
Ted Lowe (1920 - 2011)

This said, the inevitable failed to happen
John Pulman (1923 - 1998)

Griffiths is snookered on the brown, which for those of you watching in black and white, is the ball directly behind the pink.
Ted Lowe (1920 - 2011)

Compared with the jobs I used to do this is money for old rope.
Terry Griffiths (1947 -)

Whoever called snooker 'chess with balls' was rude, but right.
Clive James (1939 -)

My favorite pub game is, of course, snooker. Any game whose rules basically amount to finding a table covered in mess and slowly and methodically putting it all away out of sight is one with which I can empathise.
Jon Richardson (1982 -)

Steve, with his sip of water, part of his make-up
Ted Lowe (1920 - 2011)

He's completely disappeared. He's gone back to his dressing room, nobody knows where he has gone.
Ted Lowe (1920 - 2011)

He's lucky in one sense and lucky in the other
Ted Lowe (1920 - 2011)

A little pale in the face, but then his name is White
Ted Lowe (1920 - 2011)

If you can't find the one being hustled in the pool room, it's you.
Anon

This looks like being the longest frame in the match, even though it's the first.
Clive Everton (1937 -)

Fred Davies, the doyen of snooker, now 67 years of age and too old to get his leg over, uses his left hand instead.
Ted Lowe (1920 - 2011)

Sex at age 90 is like trying to shoot pool with a rope.
George F Burns (1896 - 1996)

CHAPTER 26: SOCCER

I never comment on referees and I'm not going to break the habit
of a lifetime for that prat.
Ron Atkinson (1939 -)

Premier League football is a multi-million pound industry with
the aroma of a blocked toilet and the principles of a knocking
shop.
Michael Parkinson (1935 -)

Of course I didn't take my wife to see Rochdale as an anniversary
present. It was her birthday. Would I have got married in the
football season? Anyway, it was Rochdale reserves.
Bill Shankley (1913 -1981)

Ah yes, Frank Sinatra. He met me once y'know?
Brian Clough (1935 - 2004)

If we can play like that every week, we'll get some level of
consistency.
Alex Ferguson (1941 -)

If you're a burglar, it's no good poncing about outside somebody's
house, looking good with your swag bag ready. Just get in there,
burgle them and come out. I don't advocate that obviously, it's
just an analogy.'
Ian Holloway (1963 -)

We didn't underestimate them but they were a lot better than we
thought.
Bobby Robson (1933 - 2009)

I am no longer Chelsea coach and I do not have to defend them
any more, so I think it is correct if I say Drogba is a diver.
Jose Mourinho (1963 -)

I couldn't be more chuffed if I were a badger at the start of the mating season.
Ian Holloway (1963 -)

Mind you, I've been here during the bad times too - one year we came second
Bob Paisley (1919 - 1996)

I know this is a sad occasion but I think that Dixie would be amazed to know that even in death he could draw a bigger crowd than Everton can on a Saturday afternoon.
Bill Shankley (1913 - 1981)

A football team is like a piano. You need eight men to carry it and three who can play the damn thing.
Bill Shankley (1913 - 1981)

I wouldn't say I was the best manager in the business. But I was in the top one.
Brian Clough (1935 - 2004)

Beckham? His wife can't sing and his barber can't cut hair.
Brian Clough (1935 - 2004)

When I go to the press conference before the game, in my mind the game has already started.
Jose Mourinho (1963 -)

If Roman Abramovich helped me out in training we would be bottom of the league and if I had to work in his world of big business, we would be bankrupt!
Jose Mourinho (1963 -)

Alan Brazil: "I was sad to hear yesterday about the death of Inspector Morse, TV's John Shaw."
Mike Parry: "John Thaw, Alan."
Alan Brazil: "Do you know; I've been doing that all morning. John, if you're listening, sorry mate

With the greatest possible respect, Luis Garcia is a tart.
Alan Brazil (1959 -)

Giroud scored a brilliant header with the last kick of the game.
Chris Kamara (1957 -)

If Everton were playing at the bottom of the garden, I'd pull the curtains.
Bill Shankley (1913 - 1981)

A lot of football success is in the mind. You must believe
you are the best and then make sure that you are. In my time at
Liverpool we always said we had the best two teams on
Merseyside, Liverpool and Liverpool Reserves.
Bill Shankley (1913 - 1981)

The best side drew.
Bill Shankley (1913 - 1981)

Who'll win the league? It's a toss of a coin between three of them.
Matt le Tissier (1968 -)

I'm not saying he's pale and thin, but the maid in our hotel room
pulled back the sheets and remade the bed without realising he
was still in it!
Brian Clough (1935 - 2004)

That lad must have been born offside.
Alex Ferguson (1941 -)

Sometimes you see beautiful people with no brains. Sometimes
you have ugly people who are intelligent, like scientists.
Jose Mourinho (1963 -)

Pressure? There is no pressure. Bird Flu is pressure. No, you
laugh, but I am being serious. I am more worried about the swan
then I am about football.
Jose Mourinho (1963 -)

If you stand still there's only one way to go, and that's backwards.
Peter Shilton (1949 -)

It is better to fail aiming high than to succeed aiming low. And we of Spurs have set our sights very high, so high in fact that even failure will have in it an echo of glory.
Bill Nicholson (1919 - 2004)

Sandro's holding his face. You can tell from that it's a knee injury.
Dion Dublin (1969 -)

He had an eternity to play that ball... but he took too long over it.
Martin Tyler (1945 -)

In his interviews, Beckham manages to sit on the fence very well and keeps both ears on the ground.
Brian Kerr (1953 -)

Some people think football is a matter of life and death. I don't like that attitude. I can assure them it is much more serious than that.
Bill Shankley (1913-1981)

If you're not sure what to do with the ball, just pop it in the net and we'll discuss your options afterwards.
Bill Shankley (1913 - 1981)

Rome wasn't built in a day. But I wasn't on that particular job.
Brian Clough (1935 - 2004)

Players lose you games, not tactics. There's so much crap talked about tactics by people who barely know how to win at dominoes.
Brian Clough (1935 - 2004)

During the afternoon it rained only in this stadium – our kitman saw it. There must be a micro-climate here. It was like a swimming pool.
Jose Mourinho (1963 -)

Barcelona is a cultural city with many great theatres and this boy [Lionel Messi] has learned very well. He's learned play-acting.
Jose Mourinho (1963 -)

Please don't call me arrogant, but I'm European champion and I think I'm a special one
Jose Mourinho (1963 -)

In the papers this morning: 'Police closing in on Ian Holloway.' Sorry... it's 'Palace closing in on Ian Holloway.
Alan Brazil (1959 -)

Paolo Di Canio is one picnic short of a hamper.
Alan Brazil (1959 -)

It's real end-to-end stuff, but unfortunately it's all up at Forest's end.
Chris Kamara (1957 -)

I don't make predictions and never will.
Paul Gascoigne (1967 -)

In 1978, between Manchester City winning one game and their next win, there had been three popes.
Frank Skinner (1957 -)

If you've got three Scots in your side, you've got a chance of winning something. If you've got any more, you're in trouble.
Bill Shankley (1913 - 1981)

Pressure is working down the pit. Pressure is having no work at all. Pressure is trying to escape relegation on 50 shillings a week. Pressure is not the European Cup or the Championship or the Cup Final. That's the reward.
Bill Shankley (1913 - 2004)

Our talking point this morning is George Best, his liver transplant and the booze culture in football. Don't forget, the best caller wins a crate of John Smith's.
Alan Brazil (1959 -)

Julian Dicks is everywhere. It's like they've got eleven Dicks on the field.
Metro Radio.

CHAPTER 27: SQUASH

Squash - that's not exercise, it's flagellation.
Noel Coward (1899 – 1973)

If you think squash is a competitive activity, try flower arranging.
Alan Bennett (1934 -)

My definition of winning at squash is playing and surviving, and I've never lost a match.
Arlen Specter

Squash is boxing with racquets.
Jonah Barrington (1941 -)

CHAPTER 28: TENNIS

Sure, on a given day I could beat him. But it would have to be a day he had food poisoning.
Mel Purcell (1959 -)

The trouble with me is that every match I play against five opponents: umpire, crowd, ball boys, court, and myself.
Goran Ivanišević (1971 -)

Ladies, here's a hint. If you're up against a girl with big boobs, bring her to the net and make her hit backhand volleys. That's the hardest shot for the well-endowed.
Billie Jean King (1943 -)

In tennis the addict moves about a hard rectangle and seeks to ambush a fuzzy ball with a modified snow-shoe.
Elliot Chaze (1915 – 90)

To err is human. To put the blame on someone else is doubles.
Anonymous

An otherwise happily married couple may turn a mixed doubles game into a scene from Who's Afraid of Virginia Woolf.
Rod Laver (1938 -)

When the Williams sisters play tennis, it gets pretty hot. When they start grunting, I'm in.
Robin Williams (1951 – 2014)

Experience is a great advantage. The problem is that when you get the experience, you're too damned old to do anything about it.
Jimmy Connors (1952 -)

The depressing thing about tennis is that no matter how good I get, I'll never be as good as a wall.
Mitch Hedberg (1968 – 2005)

It's one-on-one out there, man. There ain't no hiding. I can't pass the ball.
Pete Sampras (1971 -)

We're from the ghetto. Venus is a ghetto Cinderella. People from the ghetto don't get nervous
Richard Williams (1942 -)

A tennis racket is a trampoline for a tennis ball. My favorite score is love-all, because that's the right thing to do as a Christian and an Overpopulationist.
Jarod Kintz (1982 -)

Sex doesn't interfere with your tennis; it's staying out all night trying to find it that affects your tennis
Andre Agassi (1970 -)

It's not really a shorter skirt, I just have longer legs
Anna Kournikova (1981 -)

The difference between involvement and commitment is like ham and eggs. The chicken is involved; the pig is committed
Martina Navratilova (1956 -)

Tennis is the only sport with love in the score, and that makes it the most romantic. I would be a player, but I wisely use the net to go fishing instead.
Jarod Kintz (1982 -)

I can't believe how hard Agassi hits the ball. It's like he's got a gun. No one hit the ball like that in my day. Ion Tiriac didn't drive that fast.
Ilie Nastase (1946-)

When Ilie Nastase's winning he's objectionable. When he's losing, he's highly objectionable.
Adrian Clark

John McEnroe has hair like badly turned broccoli.
Clive James (1939 -)

Professionalism in tennis ... only resulted in making billionaires out of rude children, producing an onslaught of moody defectors, and a lot of guys with hair that looks as if bats slept in it... Meanwhile, my head swims with the thought that I have watched tennis progress from Don Budge and Alice Marble to Farrah Fawcett becoming John McEnroe's mother-in-law.
Dan Jenkins (1929 -)

The Benson and Hedges Cup was won by McEnroe ... he was as charming as always, which means that he was as charming as a dead mouse in a loaf of bread.
Clive James (1939 -)

The best doubles pair in the world is John McEnroe and anyone else.
Peter Fleming (1955 -)

Bjoring Borg ... a Volvo among tennis stars.
Peter Freedman

Everyone thinks my name is Jerry Laitis and they call me Mr Laitis. What can you do when you have a name that sounds like a disease?
Vitas Gerulaitis (1954 – 94)

Ten of the world's greatest rarities: No. 4: A British tennis player with a can of silver polish.
Journalists Mail on Sunday

The crowds at Flushing Meadow are about as impartial as a Nuremberg Rally.
Ian Wooldridge (1932 – 2007)

Mixed doubles are always starting divorces. If you play with your wife, you fight with her; if you play with somebody else, she fights with you.
Sidney Wood (1911 – 2009)

A traditional fixture at Wimbledon is the way the BBC TV commentary box fills up with British players eliminated in the early rounds.
Clive James (1939 -)

At Wimbledon, the ladies are simply the candles on the cake.
John Newcombe (1944 -)

Hardy Amies once told me that the sexiest thing he had seen was nuns playing tennis.
Prudence Glynn (1935 – 86)

I may have exaggerated a bit when I said that 80 per cent of the top women tennis players are fat pigs. It's only 75 per cent.
Richard Krajicek (1971 -)

Tennis was a game invented by a woman named Samantha Tennis in 1839, in the village of Lobsworth, County of Kent, as a diversion for the wealthy and titled Englishmen of the region, who had nothing better to do at the time but drink, belch and wear funny clothes.
Dan Jenkins (1929 -)

CHAPTER 29: WEIGHTLIFTING

I've made many good friends in bodybuilding, though there are few I'd trust to oil my back.
Lee Labrada (1960 -)

The best activities for your health are pumping and humping.
Arnold Schwarzenegger (1947 -)

Bodybuilding is my religion, the gym is my church.
Anon

Are you fat and ugly? Join our gym and just be ugly!
Anon

I believe that every human has a finite amount of heartbeats. I don't intend to waste any of mine running around doing exercises.
Neil Armstrong (1930 – 2012)

Accidentally consumed five biscuits when I wasn't paying attention. Those biscuits are wily fellows - they leap in like sugary ninjas.
Charles Dickens (1812 – 1870)

I don't exercise. If God had wanted me to bend over, he would have put diamonds on the floor.
Joan Rivers (1933 – 2014)

This is Gregoriava from Bulgaria. I saw her snatch this morning during her warm up and it was amazing. Weightlifting commentator.
Pat Glenn

I do 5 sit-ups every morning. May not sound like much, but there's only so many times you can hit the snooze button.
Anon

Exercises are like prose, whereas yoga is the poetry of movements.
Amit Ray (1960 -)

Exercise is a dirty word. Every time I hear it I wash my mouth out with chocolate.
Charles M. Schulz (1922 – 2000)

So I said to the gym instructor: 'Can you teach me to do the splits?' He said: 'How flexible are you?' I said: I can't make Tuesdays.
Tim Vine (1967 -)

Biceps are like ornaments on a Christmas tree.
Ed Coan (1963 -)

There is no reason to be alive if you can't do the deadlift!
Jon Pall Sigmarsson (1960 – 93)

If you think lifting weights is dangerous, try being weak. Being weak is dangerous.
Bret Contreras

To be number one, you have to train like you're number two.
Maurice Green (1974 -)

I found there was only one way to look thin: hang out with fat people.
Rodney Dangerfield (1921 – 2004)

I tried exercise but found I was allergic to it - my skin flushed, my heart raced, I got sweaty, short of breath. Very very dangerous.
Anon

I'm afraid the handle on your recliner chair does not count as an exercise machine.
Anon

My favorite exercise at the gym would probably be judging.
Anon

Thought of the day: If heat makes things expand...I don't have a weight problem...I'm just HOT.
Anon

Sure I have rock hard abs, I just keep them under all this fluff so people don't like me just for my body!
Anon

A stationary bike is a device that epitomizes the phrase 'hurry up and wait'.
Jarod Kintz (1982 -)

The word 'aerobics' came about when the gym instructors got together and said: If we're going to charge $10 an hour, we can't call it Jumping up and down.
Rita Rudner (1953 -)

I'm in good shape. That shape is round.
Jarod Kintz (1982 -)

CHAPTER 30: WRESTLING

Rick Steiner is so stupid, he once stayed up all night to study for a urine test.
Jim Cornette (1961 -)

I don't know what it is, but I can't look at Hulk Hogan and believe that he is the end result of millions and millions of years of evolution.
Jim Murray (1957 -)

If Mr. McMahon dies, do you think the mourners will outnumber the cheering section?
Jerry Lawler (1949 -)

I'm not crazy or weird, my reality is just different than yours.
Justin Gabriel (1981 -)

I got a tough one for you. If your mom and dad got a divorce, would they still be brother and sister? Ha, Ha! That's a tough one, isn't it?
Jerry Lawler (1949 -)

Wrestling is ballet with violence.
Jesse Ventura (1951 -)

I learned long ago, never to wrestle with a pig, you get dirty; and besides, the pig likes it.
George Bernard Shaw (1856 – 1950)

Helen Hart is the only person I know with an autographed copy of the Bible.
Jerry Lawler (1949 -)

Vince Russo destroyed the Periodic Table as he only recognises the element of surprise.
Jim Cornette (1961 -)

I'll hit you so hard you'll starve to death rolling.
Jim Garvin (1952 -)

I see Sandy Barr got himself a $4 haircut...$1 for each side.
Scott Anthony (1964 -)

If Chris Masters was any smarter, he would be an idiot.
John Layfield (1964 -)

Win if you can, lose is you must, but ALWAYS cheat!
Jesse Ventura (1951 -)

Broken necks, splattered patellas, severed arteries: These are the things from which dreams are made of.
Road Warrior Hawk (1957 – 2003)

Ric Flair, you once called me a woman. Well, what I want to know is, how does it feel to get beat by a woman?
Roddy Piper (1954 – 2015)

Samoan Savage is so ugly he has to get up early in the morning & ambush breakfast.
Jim Cornette (1961 -)

You'll find sympathy in the dictionary between shit and suicide.
Roddy Piper (1954 – 2015)

I believe that professional wrestling is clean and everything else in the world is fixed.
Frank Deford (1938 -)

Norman is so stupid; mind readers charge him half price.
Jim Cornette (1961 -)

This is the great fault of wine; it first trips up the feet: it is a cunning wrestler.
Titus Maccius Plautus (225BC – 185BC)

It's a little like wrestling a gorilla. You don't quit when you're tired-you quit when the gorilla is tired.
Robert Strauss (1913 – 75)

The way I wrestle five-year-olds makes me think if I were ever attacked by a pack of midgets, I'd be OK.
Jarod Kintz (1982 -)

Helen Hart is so old, she remembers when the Dead Sea was sick.
Jerry Lawler (1949 -)

Right out of high school I never had the fear of getting beat, which is how most people lose.
Dan Gable (1948 -)

Is that Paul Bearer's face or did his butt grow a nose?
Jerry Lawler (1949 -)

The saddest moment in a child's life is not when he learns that Santa Claus isn't real, it's when he learns that Vince Russo is.
Jim Cornette (1961 -)

He (Ahmed Johnson) has the IQ of 2 and it takes 3 just to grunt.
Jerry Lawler (1949 -)

The art of living is more like wrestling than dancing.
Marcus Aurelius (121 – 180AD)

The Rock says this, if the Rock hits you he'll kill you. If he misses, the wind behind the punch will give you pneumonia and you'll die anyway, so the choice is yours, Jabroni.
Dwayne Johnson (1972 -)

If you hung him for being a good singer, you'd be hanging an innocent man!
Gorilla Monsoon (1937 – 1999)

I'm not a racist like Brett Hart, I hate everyone equally!
Jerry Lawler (1949 -)

Rick Steiner is so stupid, it takes him 1 1/2 hours to watch `60 Minutes'.
Jim Cornette (1961 -)

You don't throw rocks at a man with a machine gun!
Roddy Piper (1954 – 2015)

He's as strong as an ox...and ALMOST as smart!
Roddy Piper (1954 – 2015)

Norman is so fat. He has furniture disease - his chest is in his drawers.
Jim Cornette (1961 -)

If Shakespeare was alive today, he would be writing wrestling shows.
Chris Jericho (1970 -)

Once you've wrestled, everything else in life is easy.
Dan Gable (1948 -)

Professional wrestling's most mysterious hold is on its audience.
Luke Neely

ONE LAST THING...

If you enjoyed this book or found it useful I'd be very grateful if you'd post a short review on Amazon. Your support really does make a difference and I read all the reviews personally so I can get your feedback and make this book even better.
If you'd like to leave a review, then all you need to do is click the review link on this book's page on Amazon.
There are also other books by the author;

The Big Book of Quotes
501 Quotes about Love
501 Quotes about Life
The Book of Best Sports Quotes
An Inspirational Quote A Day
Quotes: The Box Set

Many thanks for your support

Made in the USA
Columbia, SC
23 December 2017